To Friends of the Library:
I hope you will like reading this
story of my life.
Best Wishes & God Bless You!
Bob Dowding

A FEW SURVIVED

14
15
22

BOB DOWDING

with JULIE LISKA

Dageforde Publishing, Inc.

ISBN 1-886225-48-6
Cover design by Angie Johnson Art Productions

Library of Congress Cataloging-in-Publication Data
Dowding, Robert L., 1918-
    A few survived / Robert L. Dowding ; with Julie Liska.
    p. cm.
  ISBN 1-886225-48-6 (alk. paper)
    1. Dowding, Robert L., 1918- 2. World War, 1939-1945—Prisoners and prisons, Japanese. 3. World War, 1939-1945 Personal narratives, American. 4. Prisoners of war—Japan Biography. I. Liska, Julie.
    D805.J3 A3 1999
    940.54′7252—dc21
                                    99-35482
                                            CIP

Dageforde Publishing, Inc.
122 South 29th Street
Lincoln, Nebraska 68510
Ph: (402) 475-1123 FAX: (402) 475-1176
email: info@dageforde.com

Visit our website: www.dageforde.com

Printed in the United States of America
10 9 8 7 6 5 4 3

CKNOWLEDGMENTS

I have thought about writing my memoirs for many years. As my wife Martha has said, "It is time to quit talking and start writing."

This is primarily a story for my children and grandchildren—a story of my life and my small part in World War II. Now in my eightieth year, I have attempted to bring this story to completion. Perhaps in doing so I will remind some that America is "the land of the free and home of the brave."

Without the help of a nice young lady—a friend whom I've known for quite some time—named Julie Liska, I would not have been able to get my thoughts into words. She was patient, encouraging, and very persistent in pushing me to get busy with this story. I must say "Thank you very much, Julie."

My thanks to the *Lincoln Journal-Star*, *Seward County Independent*, the *Blue Valley Blade*, and the Seward Senior

Center, for giving me permission to use these clippings from the wartime newspapers.

And last, but not least, those friends of mine who have helped each other in War and Peace. Those men from the Hq and Hq Sq, 5th Air Base Group and attached units from 440th Ordnance Company, and 2nd Quartermaster Supply Company; among whom *A FEW SURVIVED.*

*Bob Dowding and Julie Liska at work on **A Few Survived.***

DEDICATION

I want to dedicate this book to my father, Floyd Dowding, who strongly encouraged me to take typewriting during my junior and senior years in high school, and my mother, Agnes Dowding, who walked to church every morning of my "Missing in Action" and "Prisoner of War" days so that she might be able to attend Mass and pray for me.

CONTENTS

Bob's Memories: Medals received from the United States and the Philippines. Photo at left taken in March of 1946; at right in September of 1944 as a Japanese Prisoner of War.

# PREFACE

The cover of this book is RED—Red for the blood of my friends and the many soldiers who were injured or killed in the Pacific and Europe during their efforts to keep America free.

I don't know that any of you reading this can appreciate the freedom that you have. Not until you have been a prisoner with no freedom at all can you really know how much God has blessed us here in the United States.

The photo on the cover was taken in Yokkaichi by the Japanese after our arrival from the Philippines in September 1944. We were still prisoners for a year after the photo was shot. Some of my friends were in a group who broke into the camp commander's office and found these pictures. I was glad to get this rare souvenir home to show people back in the States how tough it really was.

It is really hard for me to put into words the hunger, suffering, and mental anguish that we experienced during our prisoners of war years.

I feel that my faith in God, and the prayers of my family, helped me to survive those days of war and the years of being a prisoner of the Japanese.

Giving time and service to my community, to the St. Vincent de Paul Catholic Church, and to God is only an effort to repay for all the blessings I have received.

Yes, I've seen the worst of times and the best of times.

OOKING BACK

So much has changed since my life began in 1918 in the small southeastern Nebraska town of Seward. Much of what I knew as a boy has changed through the years. Like dust scattered by a hot July wind, the people and places once so familiar to me have been swept away to a distant place journeyed through only in memory.

Most of what I recall is pleasant—inspired by the security of my beloved family and the routine of small-town life. But in the fall of 1940, at age twenty-one, all of this would change. Events transpiring half a world away would soon draw me in and challenge all that I knew.

The world was firmly gripped by World War II. Soon, I would join the conflict as a member of the U.S. Army. And as my destiny began to take shape, I would find myself in the unrelenting grasp of the Japanese forces. As my eighty-year-old mind drifts back to that distant time spent in a POW camp, I recall the hunger,

1

fear, and constant struggle—where only *A FEW SURVIVED*.

What occurred during my imprisonment—how I dealt with it and endured—hinged on the life I knew as a boy; the post-depression era where the pace was slower and a young man's fancy could contemplate the wonders of the world from the safety of what was familiar and dear.

CHILDHOOD DAYS

I was born on November 17, 1918—five days after the World War I armistice was signed. As dusk fell over the rural Nebraska landscape, my life began in a little house located on the south side of the 1000 block of west Seward Street. My dad's mother, Emma Dowding, lived just across the street.

After a few years, we moved across the street to 1006 Seward Street. I still remember walking to school from that location. My folks paid about $15.00 a month for house rent at the time.

The agricultural community in which Seward is located was hard hit by the depression. Living in the part of the country dubbed the "Dust Bowl," those years were unlike any I've seen since.

I have many memories of those hot, summer days of my childhood. Each night, southern winds would bring red dust up from Oklahoma, covering everything in its path. There was no air conditioning, so we slept on the wooden floor of the front porch.

Some people lived in apartments above downtown businesses. Many would take a blanket and sleep out on the courthouse lawn at night because of the unbearable heat in their upstairs bedrooms. Although today this seems like an unlikely option, back then things were quite different. There was a small-town feel among Seward's 2,500 inhabitants and everybody knew everybody else. Nobody, including the city's one- or two-man police force, thought there was anything wrong with the courthouse lawn doubling as summer sleeping quarters. When the new day dawned, all were gone before those planning to do business at the courthouse arrived.

Horses were a big part of life in the early 1900s. Cars were still rare, and many city-dwellers simply walked to their destinations. For longer trips or work, however, horses were the answer.

Of course, someone was needed to clean up the mess that beasts of burden left behind. Each day at about 4 A.M., a man hired for the job went around town with a two- wheel push cart, broom, and shovel.

Horse-drawn dray wagons made regular deliveries of coal from house to house. Those beasts of burden were also responsible for pulling the city garbage collector along alleys as he performed his weekly service.

One of the more common sights was that of the ice man toting his frozen deliveries in a cart pulled by horses.

When the river froze, men chipped out blocks of ice and stored them in a warehouse for later use. Most people had some type of refrigeration system that used these blocks in either the 25- or 50-pound sizes available. Local residents would leave a sign in their windows with their order. Using a huge pair of tongs, the ice man would throw the block over his shoulder which was protected by a leather apron.

Some homes had wooden ice boxes located against an exterior wall. In that case, the ice man could simply fill it from the outside. Once delivered, the ice would slowly melt and empty into a pan located beneath the unit. The pan had to be emptied regularly or the melted remains would leak all over the floor. In about a week, it was time for another delivery.

The only thing that equaled the blistering days of summer were the bitterly cold winters. Snow from downtown city streets was hand-shoveled into carts pulled by horses. Often, just a narrow strip of sidewalk was cleared. The drifts on each side would be several feet high.

Because it was a small town and everyone was acquainted, we were all familiar with a couple of colorful men who walked the streets. One older man spent his summer days pushing a wheelbarrow of vegetables around town. Another was well known for trading knives—sight unseen. Taking him up on his offer could mean becoming the owner of a knife with no blade!

Money was scarce and many had lost their farms because of the low prices offered for grain and livestock.

Still, those living in the city had to deal with equally difficult financial hardships.

My father, Floyd Dowding, had no interest in farming. Instead, he managed to secure a position at the local post office in about 1917. Even though it was a decent job, postal workers were given time off without pay during the darkest days of the depression.

To earn a little extra money, Dad would purchase some balloons or other novelties and set up stands at community celebrations in Seward and neighboring towns.

With the whole family pitching in, we sold orangeade (mixed up in a 20- or 30-gallon crock jar) for 5 cents a drink. The novelties and balloons sold for 5 or 10 cents each. All the while, Mom and Dad kept an eye on us and the merchandise.

When I got a little older, I remember the whole family fishing at the Blue River. At that time the river ran clean without chemical pollution.

After Dad got off work each day between 4:00 and 4:30, we would grab some old cane poles and worms for bait, pile into the old car, and head for the river. We would spend hours by the Big Blue. My mother, Agnes (Zeleny), also really enjoyed fishing. She usually had some sandwiches ready and we had those for supper. At the time, there were no activities for kids, and fishing provided an inexpensive form of entertainment.

Mom was a good cook and always prepared what we caught for a meal. During the summer, the fish might replace our usual meal of a minced ham sandwich. In the winter, we usually dined on corn meal mush for supper and fried the leftovers for breakfast the next morning. The fruits and vegetables we ate had been canned by Mom during the summer months. On Sunday, we splurged by having a roast with vegetables. Dessert was nearly always Jell-o® with a banana in it. Occasionally, Mom would buy a live guinea hen or a chicken for 25 cents. Both were good eating.

Sometimes Mom would give me 25 cents to go up-town to buy a loaf of bread for 10 cents and 15 cents worth of cold meat for sandwiches. Lunch stands around town sold hamburgers for 5 cents each or 6 for a quarter.

Forms of entertainment in those days were limited. My parents sometimes got together with a few others for a game of cards. Through Dad's long association with the local volunteer fire department and his job as mail carrier, he knew a lot of people and was quite social.

Every Saturday night we listened to the Lucky Strike Hit Parade on the radio. They played all the latest hit songs. Each Saturday in the summer, Seward held a free band concert at the courthouse square.

Going out for the evening was a family affair — there was no such thing as babysitters. When my parents attended a community dance, we sat on benches along a porch surrounding the Seward dance hall. There were screened openings around the floor so we could watch the dancing and hear the music.

Although the old dance hall is now gone, I can still remember watching couples as they glided in pairs across the floor. Many different bands came to play, including Lawrence Welk and our own local orchestra led by Ted Hughes. I don't think I ever did actually try to dance until I got out of high school.

The swimming pool, which has managed to survive through the years, was located just south of the old dance hall. It looks much the same today as it did in my youth. My brothers, sisters, and I spent almost every summer afternoon at the pool. It sported two large slides which provided us with hours of fun. Although it did have some type of filtration system, the pool had to be emptied and refilled every three or four weeks to stay ahead of the algae.

My uncle, Bill Dowding, gave swimming lessons at the pool for years and I was one of his students. Today, it bears the name of Dowding Municipal Pool, in honor of the man who devoted so much time to teaching the young.

When I was quite young, I spent a good deal of time at my grandparents in Seward. My dad's parents, James and Emma Dowding, were both natives of England. Although it was quite unusual at that time, the two divorced and my grandmother remarried James Fairbrother. They lived just a few blocks away on West Seward Street.

The Fairbrothers had a barn that housed a couple of horses. Their property also had a well from which water was drawn with a bucket. In the summer, butter and milk were lowered down the well to keep it cool.

When I got older, my family began making frequent Sunday trips to visit Grandma and Grandpa Zeleny. Going there was an all-day affair. They lived on a farm about forty-five miles south of Seward, somewhere between Swanton and Western. Dad drove an old, open touring car that had four half-doors, four seats, a roof, and no windows. It was air conditioned all right—the wind blew right through it!

The Zeleny's raised a few cows, ducks, geese, and a lot of grapes for homemade wine. During our weekly visits, Grandma always made a big dinner that included either chicken or roast beef, mashed potatoes with gravy, and all the fixings.

Both Grandma and Grandpa Zeleny were from Czechoslovakia and spoke no English. All of their children spoke both English and Czech; however, my mother never taught us the Czech language.

There were lots of interesting things to do at the farm. They had a pond where we used to play. It was quite a distance from the house and we had to walk down a ravine—which seemed more like the Grand Canyon—to get there. When they were in season, we picked grapes and strawberries. They also had bees, and sometimes we got a little honey.

During one of our visits, I decided to use the mechanical sheller to shell a couple of ears of corn for the chickens. Instead, I ended up getting the middle finger on my right hand caught in the gears. The old sheller really split it open, but they took me into Western and an old doctor sewed it up. My finger was saved, but I still have a good scar to remind me of the experience.

Occasionally, I would stay over at Grandma and Grandpa Zelenys during harvest. They did not have electricity or running water, but we hardly noticed — except on wash day.

Washing clothes without the benefit of modern conveniences was indeed difficult. Grandma had an old washing machine equipped with a lever. The lever had to be pulled back and forth to agitate clothes in the tub. Running the lever often became my job. Of course, everything was hung out on the clothesline to dry.

When my parents thought we were old enough to handle a longer trip, they decided to venture still farther. Mom's sister Emma and her husband Ed Nelson lived near a little town called Moorefield located about twenty-five miles southwest of Gothenburg. It was really out in the "boondocks" with terrible roads, hills, and canyons. Uncle Ed was trying to farm there, but it was a losing proposition. When we arrived, they told us kids to be sure and stay on the porch because there were a lot of rattlesnakes in the yard. That was the last time we ever went out there.

Back at home, I spent my days playing with kids in the neighborhood. Everyone would join in games of hide and seek and "Shinny." Shinny was a game similar to hockey but we used tree branches for clubs and a small milk can for a puck. Even though the equipment was improvised, we had lots of fun.

Later on, the other boys and I played a game called mumblety-peg. This game of skill consisted of accurately throwing a knife at a target. A knife was important to a boy in those days. In addition to games and whittling, a knife was needed to cut fishing line and clean the fish. Marble games were also popular, and the stakes ran high. Marbles were played for keeps and I still have a box of my "winnings" from these games.

In the winter, our interests changed to different activities. We frequently ice skated down on the old bayou which was located on South 8th Street, across the railroad tracks. My friends and I spent of lot of time at the little pond. There was a warming house nearby run by a man called "Shug" Miers.

When we weren't skating, we gathered into teams for a game of hockey. The river flowed along this area but we were given strict orders to stay off. The ice there was not as stable as on the old pond.

In both summer and winter, we would often go out in the evening to cut wood. Everyone knew someone with a patch of land and some trees. My dad had an agreement with a man who owned land one mile west and half-mile south of Seward. Because there were many dead trees on the parcel, all we really needed to do was collect the fallen branches and cut them up. Many trips were made there with the touring car, which we piled high with wood during each visit.

When we got to Seward, we would unload it in the yard until there was time to cut it into smaller pieces and carry it downstairs. I didn't have to worry about getting bored by not having anything to do. Whether it was after school or during the weekend, preparing wood for use was a never-ending task.

That came to an abrupt end in the early 30s. Natural gas became available in town and many, including my family, upgraded heating and cooking equipment to utilize this new luxury. Prior to that time, our heating sources consisted of a cook stove that used cobs or wood and a round heating stove in the living room. After getting heating fuel, we relied on a furnace that supplied air through a single register on the main floor. Heat rose to the upper bedroom levels through a ceiling grate.

Eliminating wood also had another advantage — there was no longer any need to empty ashes from furnaces and stoves.

At the time natural gas came on the scene, electricity was already commonly used in Seward. Washing machines, irons, radios, and electric lights were in almost every home.

Indoor plumbing was also common. Water could be obtained through a hand pump for drinking. For washing, many homes had a cistern that collected rain water. These large, underground collection tanks were between eight- and ten-feet deep and constructed of cement or brick. Shaped like a narrow-necked bottle, they were also quite dangerous. Small children were known to fall in, become trapped, and drown.

Although cisterns had disadvantages, they were largely seen as an improvement. However, the introduction of natural gas greatly surpassed other innovations of the time and made everyone's lives a little easier.

Along with my many fond childhood memories are the many enjoyable times I spent in school. I always liked learning something new, so I looked forward to going to kindergarten. During my first year, I received a little book because I was neither absent nor tardy a single day. I still have this treasure, entitled *A Child's Garden of Verses* which I received in 1924.

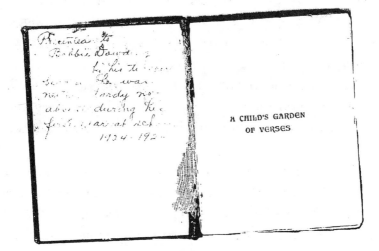

A Child's Garden of Verses,
a gift from Bob's teacher for perfect attendance, 1924.

Pocket knife a gift from the Seward Rotary Club, 1932.

I did a lot of reading at the library and at home. When I skipped the fourth grade, I was able to keep up with the fifth graders.

Imagine my pride when, at the end of eighth grade, I was given a Rotary Club Award — a pearl-handled knife, for having the highest grade of any boy in my class. The Rotary Club award was something I treasured throughout the remainder of my school years. The marbles, knife, and book of poems are some of my dearest possessions because of the fond memories they invoke.

Like school, church was an important part of my life. Each Sunday and on religious holidays, my family could be found attending Mass in the wood-framed Catholic Church on the corner of 3rd and Seward Streets. We were joined by 35 or 40 others while worshiping in the town's original Catholic structure. On Christmas, we always walked to midnight mass.

I became an altar boy at about age ten and continued to serve until graduating from high school. Soon after I started, I learned just how tricky this job can be. While lighting candles surrounding the Christmas nativity scene, I leaned over and caught my sleeve on fire. I calmly put it out, but it did cause quite a bit of excitement in the church.

The celebration of special events was marked by modest gift exchanges. One year especially stands out. Dad always enjoyed hunting, so he bought me a little 410 gauge shotgun when I turned fifteen, and I was on my way to becoming a hunter. I was able to shoot some pheasant, rabbits, and squirrels from time to time. Of course, all these went on the dinner table.

Other holidays, including Christmas, did not center on gift-giving although, as children, we did get one or two special things. Two of the most memorable were a set of Tinker Toys and an erector set. I enjoyed playing with both for years after receiving them.

We celebrated Independence Day, Thanksgiving, Christmas, and New Year's Day. We always had goose for dinner on New Year's Day.

I tried to help my parents out financially when I could. Between my junior and senior years of high school, I found a job with a road paving project between Seward and York, a town located about 26 miles west. I would fill a three-gallon bucket with water in Tamora and ride to the work site in one of the little dump trucks they used in those days. I received pay of 15 cents an hour. The trucks would pick up a load of dry cement and sand and haul it to the work site where it was mixed in a machine and poured out onto the road bed. All the work of readying the road bed and leveling the cement was done by hand. Toting the three-gallon tin can and dipper, I walked along where the men were working to give them a drink. They all drank from the same dipper, completely unconcerned about germs as we would be today.

There were also a lot of other jobs. One was at the Seward Bakery working for Mr. Henry Wehr. I would go to work at about 5:00 A.M. to wash bread pans, sweep the floor, and wash windows. I quit about 8:00 A.M. so that I could get to school on time. The pay for my effort was one sack of day-old rolls that I took home for my family to enjoy. This was considered a good wage at the time.

I also worked as a shoe-shine boy for several barber shops. Charlie Winegar's shop was located under the Lester Jewelry store, and Les Headlee's shop was downstairs at the old Windsor Hotel (located where the Jones National Bank is now).

Most of my business came from downtown businessmen or local residents who wanted to get slicked up on Saturday. Many got their shoes shined while waiting to get a haircut. Once in a while I got a tip, but for the most part my total profit was about a nickel a shine. Earning a dollar for twenty shines was doing pretty good.

Carrying ashes from the basement of a downtown men's clothing store also provided me with about 15 cents. Once a month on Saturday morning, I went door to door in Seward and in neighboring towns to deliver show bills for local movie theaters. In return, I got a few tickets to the shows which took place every evening and on Saturday and Sunday afternoons.

For a time, there were three movie theaters in downtown Seward. One was located in what is now Wirthels

Jewelry Store and another at the current location of Fabric Fair. The Rivoli Theater is still in use today. Early on, dialogue was printed on the screens. Unlike some movie houses, those in Seward did not have piano players to accompany the show's action. The price to get in was 10 cents for kids and 25 cents for adults.

I found these various jobs just by asking. There may have been others, but these I remember. Whatever I made, I gave to my parents—even though it wasn't much—to help out with expenses. Although times were difficult, I felt a sense of responsibility to earn some money where I could, but I still found time to enjoy growing up.

For many, money was a serious concern. Because we were just coming out of the dust bowl, it was not really a prosperous time. Many struggled to keep their families comfortably fed and clothed.

In high school, I joined the Boy Scouts and got much pleasure out of it. I was always a nature lover and enjoyed outdoor activities. Earl Scott, a bachelor and substitute mail carrier, was our Scoutmaster. He took us on cookouts, hiking, and, of course, fishing. I learned where the different star constellations were and how to tell time without a watch. Little did I realize that someday my knowledge would help make some sense out of my life when everything else was foreign and out of control.

We lived across the street from Russ Summers who published the *Blue Valley Blade* newspaper. He was also manager of the local adult Blue Valley League baseball team. He was an active player and often took me along to games in Seward and neighboring towns.

Many people who lived in rural areas attended nearby country schools. At that time, there was about one school on every section. If students from these locations wanted to go on to high school, they had to take county entrance exams at the end of their eighth-grade year under supervision of the County School Superintendent. This was to ensure they were academically prepared. Because Seward had a high school and I was already enrolled in junior high, it was never necessary for me to take one of these tests.

High School Days circa 1935.

Ninth graders typically took algebra, English and manual training, which was a kind of shop class similar to vocational agriculture. Tenth grade brought studies in geometry. Other classes included general agriculture (which consisted of studying different animal breeds) and Latin. Of the classes offered, I enjoyed math, spelling, and geography most. In English, we studied Shakespeare and other classics.

As I entered Seward High School, there were some choices about classes to take. My father suggested I learn shorthand and typing. It was not typical at that time for men to take either. But while delivering mail, Dad had noticed businessmen at the courthouse plucking away at their manual typewriters. Compared to my father's postal job, which often forced him to deal with heat, rain, and bitter Nebraska winters, these office jobs appeared quite comfortable. So, as I embarked upon my junior year, one or two other young men and I set out to learn some office skills. I discovered I wasn't the best in shorthand, but I did take to typing.

Later, this knowledge would be a pivotal point in determining my fate. The skill helped as early as my first day in the Army because it allowed me to work in the recruiting office rather than the infantry. At Fort Douglas, Utah, typing directed me to base headquarters rather than some other detail. In the Philippines, my ability sent me to Japanese headquarters rather than the rice fields several times.

Graduation, May, 1936.

Time passed, and eventually my high school days drew to a close. Sixty-six classmates and I prepared to become Seward Public High School's graduating class of 1936.

We had significantly different expectations of graduation than people do today. The occasion was not marked with the publication of a yearbook. None of us had money to spend on such an item because of the hard times. For me, one of the high points was receiving a new gray suit, in which my graduation picture was taken and I later wore to the ceremony. Ordered from the J.C. Penney Catalog, the purchase price was a hefty $10.00. To make it worth our money, the company threw in a free shirt and tie. In those days, a new shirt was worth about 79 cents.

The graduation ceremony took place on a recently completed open-air stage called the Band Shell. Located at the corner of Jackson Avenue and North 5th Street in Seward, the Band Shell was filled to capacity with friends and family of the sixty-seven Seward High School graduates.

As I look back on my childhood and life as a young adult, I'd say that, all in all, things were pretty good. Others did not have it so easy. In those days you would read about bread and soup lines in the big cities. In my small town, the local welfare office helped out the poor. And when the older folks were down and out, they went to the County Poor Farm.

Seward County's poor farm was located in a neat two-story building south of town. Those who could help out in some way did jobs like helping to tend the garden.

To ease the financial stress of American citizens, President Roosevelt instituted the "New Deal." With the goal of creating some type of employment for hard-hit Americans, the Works Projects Administration (WPA) and Civilian Conservation Corps (CCC) were formed.

The WPA provided men with work that facilitated community improvements. The dance hall in nearby Bee, Nebraska, was built by the WPA as were many outhouses for county schools. Young men went off to the Civilian Conservation Corps (CCC) where they worked in National Parks and various forested areas. These jobs helped men earn a few extra dollars to feed their families.

But as for me, there were no missed meals, and we all lived life at a leisurely pace.

LEAVING CHILDHOOD BEHIND

After graduation, the rich went off to college, and the rest of us set out to find work. Many of the women became housekeepers. Because country schools were so prevalent at the time, teaching was also a commonly sought profession for women. Men, on the other hand, simply found work wherever they could.

As for me, whenever I had a chance to make a nickel, I did. Immediately after graduation I took a job at the Jerpe Commission Company as a bookkeeper. The business specialized in buying truckloads of live chickens from nearby farmers which were dressed at our plant. The chickens were then packed in ice and loaded on rail cars destined for distant city locations.

When the office work slowed down, I worked out in the plant as a "honey boy," which was a nice name for a stinky job. I shoveled manure out of cages the chickens were held in and hauled it by wheelbarrow to a truck waiting outside. When the truck was full, somebody else drove it away.

Saturdays were especially busy, since that was when farmers would come in to sell their cream and eggs. On that day, I helped at the uptown cream and egg buying station. "Pop" Fillinger was in charge there and taught me to test cream (to determine the butterfat content) and to candle eggs to see if they were spoiled. To test cream content, a sample of milk was put in an electric machine that spun around rapidly. Centrifugal force separated the heavier cream from the lighter milk, making it possible to easily gauge the amount of cream in the sample. Eggs were spot-checked when customers brought them in to ensure freshness. A couple were put in a machine with rear illumination. Spoiled or fertile eggs would have dark centers, while those acceptable for cooking were clear. All the time I was with Jerpe, the wage was 20 cents per hour.

Later, this plant experimented with freezing dressed chickens. The company was purchased by the big Swanson Food company in Omaha when the frozen food business was getting started.

In the summer of 1937, the Fairmont Creamery opened an ice cream store in Seward and I got a job there. It was located on the north side of the Seward County courthouse, west of what is now Brockhoff Drug. Customers could pick from fourteen different flavors of ice cream. At the time, double-dip ice cream cones were 5 cents and an "overflow" pint was 15 cents.

I really thought I had a good job when I went to work for Henriksen Grocery that fall. It was my first permanent, full-time job and offered some hope of continued future employment. My jobs consisted of delivering groceries in a Model A panel truck, sweeping the floor, washing windows, stocking shelves, and whatever else needed to be done.

Since we were still in a depression, money was scarce. Many folks charged their groceries with plans of paying for them later. Unfortunately, some got in so deep that they never did get their bill paid. Mr. Henriksen helped out a lot of folks, but never did get all the money he was owed.

While at Henriksen's, I would work from 7:00 A.M. to 6:00 P.M. On Saturdays, I worked from 7:00 A.M. until 11:00 P.M. There were no eight-hour days or forty-hour weeks at that time. My pay was $1.00 a day and $2.00 per week credit on my folks' grocery bill.

Many farmers felt that after five days of work they were ready for some relaxation. By now, cars were becoming common and better transportation meant more frequent trips into town. Each Saturday, members of rural areas loaded their vehicles with whatever they had to sell and set out on their weekly trip to the county seat. It was an opportunity to visit, get groceries, and possibly catch a movie. As for those of us living in the city, everybody recognized Saturday as a special day to get dressed up and it was *the* day to do business.

While local residents were enjoying better and increased transportation, others took it to the extreme and made it a way of life. No story of the 30s would be complete without mentioning the "hoboes."

We lived just up the hill from the railroad, so I spent a lot of time down by the tracks. The hoboes would ride through on slow-moving freight trains. I don't think they had a particular destination in mind; they just kept on moving. Sometimes, a bum would get off the train and venture away from the tracks, going door to door for food. If they found a good house, it would be secretly marked so that those who followed would know where to get a sandwich.

These fellows led a dangerous life, getting on and off the trains as they moved through town. I can remember at least two who were killed. One apparently lost his footing and fell into the river. At the time, I was working at Jerpes, which was located nearby. I saw the unfortunate hobo's body floating in the water. Another time, one slipped near the depot and was cut in half as a train ran over him.

Although I didn't have anything to do with the hoboes, they did offer a rare look at life outside my small hometown. For the most part, though, I remained a naive country boy. World events outside my small town life didn't really have that much meaning to me.

People in the stores talked about a possible draft being imposed on eighteen-year-olds but they were generally unconcerned. A sense of patriotism dominated most discussions rather than debates of whether American involvement overseas was right or wrong.

Hitler's 1939 invasion of Poland went largely unnoticed by me. But America's interest in becoming involved in this affair became more apparent in September, 1940, when all young men were asked to register in case a draft would be necessary.

At the time, I was working for the City Meat Market. Because I was interested in the welfare of my community, I decided to join the local volunteer fire department. And with an eye on the future, I also took a civil service test with hopes of getting a job at the post office.

Given the rather nonchalant atmosphere of the time, I was surprised when my cousin and good friend, Max Slonecker, announced he would be going to Lincoln to join the Navy. When he invited me to ride along, I was naturally thrilled. I'd only been to the capital city a few times in my life up to that point. I was ready for some excitement, so we set out on the twenty-five-mile journey to Lincoln, Nebraska.

In those days, most of the commerce took place in downtown Lincoln. Between the University of Nebraska and the state government, many people were drawn to the city. The Haymarket area was quite prosperous and housed several wholesale businesses.

We found the Navy recruiter located in the same building as the post office. He gave us a good pep talk on what that branch of the service had to offer. By the time he finished, Max was not the only one convinced to join up. I was ready to sign on the dotted line when the recruiter dashed my hastily made plans. He informed me that nobody below 120 pounds was allowed to enlist, and I fell short weighing in at just 112 pounds.

After we left the Navy office and prepared to go home, I noticed the Army recruiter was just next door. Curious, I decided to see what he had to say.

The Army recruiter had a speech much like the Navy's, and again I was interested. But the Army also had a 120-pound weight minimum, and I could feel my chances to join an armed service slipping away. But the recruiter was not deterred. Instead, he told me to just write in 120 pounds on the enlistment form.

With that, in October, 1940, I was committed to three years in the United States Army. Lured by the promise of free room and board and a chance to travel, I never thought twice about the obligation I'd just taken on. Still naive, I never dreamed my tour of duty would far exceed three years, or that it would take me so far from home.

Photo taken in October of 1940 at time of enlistment

I had discussed the possibility of signing up with an armed force with my parents before leaving for Lincoln, so they were not surprised when I arrived home with news of my enlistment. Realizing I was twenty-one and ready to be out on my own, they didn't object.

Many in the area had already joined the local National Guard. They had drills once a month or so and got a payment each time. But being in the Guard gave those enlisted no control over where they would end up should war break out. By signing up with the Army, I felt as though I had some say in my future should military conflict occur.

So it was that I found myself swept away from the slow, quiet life of Seward to that of being a soldier. Just one day after signing up, I was packed and ready to begin my new career. I bid farewell to my family, including sisters Velma, then nineteen, Betty, fifteen, and brothers Don, aged twelve, and Dick, just four. Full of anticipation for what was to come, I boarded a bus headed for Lincoln without much thought about looking back.

THE JOURNEY BEGINS

In Lincoln, I met the Army recruiter who signed me up. He told me my orders were to report to Fort Crook, now known as the Strategic Air Command (SAC) in Bellevue, Nebraska. Two or three other newly enlisted men and I shared the ride down.

After being interviewed and settling in, they asked if any of us could type and I was the only one who could. After demonstrating my skills, I was informed that I would be starting at the Army Recruiting Office in downtown Omaha. Wearing the title of Clerk, I began typing up enlistment records, doing some letter writing, and filing.

So began my Army life—without one day of basic training.

The position in the recruiting office went smoothly, and I had no regrets about my decision to enlist. Christmas of 1940 neared and I was able to get a week off. It was good to be home for a few days. As the holiday season wrapped up, I returned to Omaha and my job of helping young men enlist in the Army.

As the dreary winter months wore on, I began feeling a little nervous. I had been an enlisted man for almost six months but had seen none of the excitement and travel the recruiter had promised. In the spring, we were trained to talk up a new branch of the Army, called the Army Air Corps, which was coming on strong. It sounded so good that I applied to transfer to the 5th Air Base Group at Fort Douglas, Utah. Again, I was excited at the possibility of some travel and seeing new sights.

After arriving at Fort Douglas, I was assigned to base headquarters doing typing and filing. Shortly after getting settled in at my new job, we were told that a new branch of the Army Air Corps was being organized called the Flying Cadets. This program would actually teach us how to fly airplanes. Sounding pretty glamorous, I filled out the application and started the other necessary paper work.

But as many know, the wheels of government turn rather slowly. In September, we got orders to prepare to go on a secret mission called *PLUM*. That was the last I heard of the Flying Cadet program.

During the summer of 1941, I had some leave coming so I went home for a week. Dad had purchased a used Model A Ford coupe with a rumble seat. He agreed to let me drive this back to Fort Douglas so that I would be able to come home again sometime. The car was real nice to have, since we could drive it to Salt Lake City, see the sites and later go swimming in the Great Salt Lake.

In August, my mother and sister Velma came to visit me at my new base. With some leave time available, the plan was for me to show them around town and Fort Douglas and then drive them back home in the Model A.

Eventually, we did get started for home. Unfortunately, my luck did not hold out. We hadn't gone far into Wyoming when the car stopped running for some strange reason. The problem was beyond my mechanical ability.

We were near Little America, which was then just a truck stop out in the middle of the desert. It was there that I made a deal with the man running the station at Little America. He said the bus stopped there, and he would give me $25.00 which would buy one-way tickets for Mom and Velma to go home. He would get the Model A, and I would hitchhike to Seward.

I guess the good Lord was smiling on me because the first ride I got took me nearly to Seward. After my visit, I hitchhiked back to Fort Douglas. That was to be my last trip home until after the war, some four years later.

Back at Fort Douglas, rumors were hot about mission *PLUM*. We had to ship all of our extra clothes and belongings home or dispose of them. One of my friends at Fort Douglas was Victor Chirnside. His folks lived at Fairbury which is just about fifty miles south of Seward. They were coming to Fort Douglas for his things and they agreed to take my belongings home to Seward.

My parents were thankful the Chirnsides were able to bring my things back and continued to correspond with them during the war. The sad part of the story is that Victor went down with the ship that was sunk by American submarines off the coast of Mindanao in 1944.

When we finally got all of our gear and equipment packed, we left by train for San Francisco. The trip took several days but, one evening, we finally arrived at the coast. We unloaded right near the docks and immediately boarded a waiting ship called *The Hugh IL. Scott.* By then, we realized our destination was probably not just down the road. It wasn't until years later that we would decode the mysterious code word *PLUM* and understand our destination was the Philippine Luzon Mindanao region.

There were approximately 160 of us from the 5th Air Base Group. Joining us were attached units of the 440th Ordnance Company and the 2nd Quartermaster Supply Detachment. Also aboard was the 192nd tank company from Kentucky, which consisted of about 200 men. Those in charge seemed to be hustling us right along. There was a sense of urgency in getting us aboard quickly. Immediately after boarding, we set sail for our mysterious and, as yet, unknown destination.

We passed under the Golden Gate Bridge at sunset. It was the first time I had seen this west coast landmark.

This was the first sea voyage for many of those on board, including myself. Prior to that time, my experience on water consisted of a small rowboat used for fishing on the river and ponds near Seward, Nebraska.

We wondered if we would get seasick and, as the choppy coastal waters bounced us around, we quickly got our answer. Soon, a number of us were lined up along the ship's rail tossing our supper to the fish. We heaved until there was no more to throw up.

Morning brought another beautiful day and we realized that we had survived our first night aboard the vessel. After walking around for an hour or two, we finally got our sea legs and felt we could move in comfort.

Remember, this was not a cruise ship. We had our bunks stacked four high somewhere down in the ship's hold. Although we did have freedom to move about the ship, we did not really mingle with the tank group. We stayed within our own circle and not on the upper deck with the officers.

Many played cards to help pass the time. When we got around to playing poker, it didn't take long for me to learn that some of those guys were pretty sharp card players. I dropped out of the game in a hurry when I realized the dealers were slick enough to know what cards the rest of us were holding.

Five or six days later, we arrived in Honolulu, Hawaii. After docking, we were allowed to go ashore. We were told not to talk too much about who we were or where we were going.

We were all pretty relaxed and used our time to wander around town. Of course, we stopped to try a few of those exotic drinks. Later, I took a tour around the island and saw all the sights, including Diamond Head, a Mormon Temple, Wheeler Field (where all the planes were lined up in neat rows), and finally, Pearl Harbor. Later, upon hearing of the Japanese attack on Pearl Harbor, I could imagine the wreckage and havoc as gunfire and bombs hit the area.

Our time in Hawaii drew to a close after four or five days. We re-boarded our ship and began sailing west. Upon departing, we thought it was unusual that our boat was accompanied by a cruiser. There was also no smoking allowed on deck after dark. We all agreed that uncovering the guns as we approached a lone, unidentified ship indicated a high level of alert, though we didn't know what to make of it at the time. We didn't realize it, but some of our people must have had the suspicion that war was close at hand. We had no idea the United States was already preparing for conflict and the Japanese were undoubtedly tracking our movement across the ocean.

After two weeks at sea, our ship docked at Manila, the Philippine capital. We were taken by truck to Fort McKinley, a short distance outside the city. The next day was Thanksgiving. We had high hopes for a good turkey dinner with all the trimmings. Instead, we ended up with plates of sauerkraut and wieners.

Our stay at the Fort McKinley military base was short, lasting only a week. We were then taken back to the docks and loaded on an inter-island boat that took us about 300 miles. On December 1, 1941, we reached our fi-

Bob Dowding

At Del Monte plantation by Building C at the edge of the pineapple field. Crates for pineapples in the background.
Dowding is in the front row in the middle.

nal destination—the city of Bugo located on the north shore of Mindanao Island in the Philippines.

This was a port where the Del Monte Corporation shipped out pineapple. We were moved by truck some miles inland and uphill to a plateau. Here, Del Monte had huge fields of pineapple. We were instructed to clean off a rather large pasture-like area and make a clearing suitable to use as an air base.

We busied ourselves with removing the brush and setting up the tents that would be our shelters. We were told additional equipment, including guns and ammunition, would arrive on the next incoming ship. As time passed and no ship arrived, we slowly began to realize we were more or less on our own.

We were told to stay out of the pineapple fields or we would be in trouble. On December 7, 1941, we received news of the Japanese bombing at Pearl Harbor and the declaration of war. Now we knew that no more ships would be coming with supplies and help.

For the first time, we realized how far away home really was and everybody felt a little nervous.

The Army Air Corps flew in sixteen B-17s from Clark Field located near Manila. The airfield had been bombed by the Japanese. Our makeshift airfield on the Del Monte land was the only alternative. Some of the planes were damaged but salvageable. We removed the machine guns from the planes that were beyond repair to use in case of an attack.

Other than these brief distractions, nothing happened. The lengthy silence took on a rather sinister feeling.

We later dug some gun placements, or pits, and mounted these ma-

Author Bob Dowding at Del Monte Airfield in machine gun pit at the start of the war. B-17 plane in background. December 9, 1941.

chine guns as best we could. I was stationed in one of the machine gun pits for about two weeks. Then I came down with one of the most common ailments in the Philippines — malaria. I was in the camp hospital which was little more than a separate tent. My illness lasted for about a week. When I recovered, I went back to headquarters to work as a typist.

Part of my job was to create a weekly newsletter that kept everyone up-to-date on what was happening. I was also assigned to keep watch for a couple of hours every night. If we had been attacked, there really wasn't much we could have done. But the rationale was that maybe a guard could somehow prevent everyone from getting wiped out in their sleep.

Christmas Eve, 1941, arrived. We celebrated the holiday in a small Catholic church in the Tankulan barrio. I

The Catholic Church in Tankulan. (The General Supplies Tent was back of the tree on the left.) Taken by author in December, 1941.

Buss Cline and Bob Dowding by their grass shack home in Tankulan, Mindanao. December 24, 1941.

served as an altar boy for the Mass, just as I had done many times while growing up.

Soldiers from a number of different units joined in the service. Some had found some native liqueur and became quite drunk. One of them was in such bad shape the priest refused to give him communion. He was told to return in the morning to receive the sacrament.

Everything at our Mindanao camp was disorganized. I did my work in a large, open building that looked like an old hay shed. The tin-roofed structure provided protection from frequent rain showers that hit the area during the wet season.

The building itself was shaped like a cross and came to be known by that name. The area where I worked was piled high with empty pineapple crates while another area of the building was used as a bunk house. Our radio equipment was housed in a trailer parked under some trees.

I took my orders from First Sergeant Parks. He was a husky man who had a military stance. He knew what he was doing and let us know he was boss. Many in my camp thought he was tough, but since I worked mostly inside, I got to see the good side of him more than most.

The day of December 19, 1941, dawned sunny and clear. As we were going about our usual mid-day business, we suddenly heard the buzz of airplanes. Looking to the southeast, I saw a number of planes high in the sky. For a moment we thought these might be American planes coming to help us. Distracted by the bombers, we failed to see fighter planes that simultaneously approached from the north. As they came closer, the horror of what was happening suddenly became very clear. All of the aircraft bore the unmistakable red fireball that was the Japanese insignia.

As bullets began hitting the area, we scrambled for whatever cover we could find. We had dug a few foxholes prior to the attack, but had little interest since we really didn't understand what they were for. In addition, the ground was hard and we didn't have good shovels with which to dig. I quickly learned to appreciate the protection the foxholes had to offer. For this first attack, I didn't even make it to a foxhole. Instead, I scrambled for a sloped area near the edge of the air field.

With no guns or ammunition to speak of, we were completely unable to defend ourselves. After about ten or fifteen minutes of strafing, all planes on the makeshift Mindanao landing field were destroyed. Next the bombers moved in, shaking the ground each time one of their deadly bombs exploded.

In all, the attack probably lasted no more than thirty minutes. When the dust settled, we discovered an officer and an enlisted man from Louisiana perished in the raid. We then knew the Japanese meant business—we knew they wanted us dead, and the war was no longer taking place in some distant place. Now, it was at our front door.

We examined the destruction. The airfield, which was about one mile long and half a mile wide, was in need of repair. We eventually realized we would have to

*A December, 1941, New Year's greeting
to Bob Dowding from his mother.*

remove the destroyed planes from the airstrip and fill in the bomb craters so the runway could be used if and when necessary. When we finished, we resumed our activities as though nothing out of the ordinary had happened.

After this initial bombing raid, the Japanese apparently decided we were not a great threat. For the most part, they left us alone and conducted only a few nuisance raids. Meanwhile, our response was to move our tents back into the jungle so they wouldn't be such obvious targets. Then, we just sat there and waited for something significant to occur.

As fate would have it, I suffered another bout of malaria. I was down for one week, occasionally experiencing periods of delirium. For two more weeks, I was too weak to do much of anything. I got whatever medication was available at the time — probably quinine. Fortunately, this was the last time I was hit by the disease.

While recovering, I was assigned to work in the office. However, I still took my turn standing guard. Everybody knew we were in a precarious situation.

Between December 19 and March 25, many Philippine natives decided to abandon their villages and seek cover in the jungle. Prior to that time, we had frequent dealings with the native girls. Some would do the soldier's laundry. Other more enterprising individuals made fried bananas or a doughnut-like food we could purchase. But after the bombings, locals felt it would be better to take their chances in the jungle than meet up with the Japanese.

Along with the native girls, some Americans were engaged in a variety of non-war activities. For example, some were involved in mining, lumbering, and shipping. A few older men had married Philippine girls and lived in the area. Many knew the terrain and later formed the basis for guerrilla forces in the area. These people harassed the Japanese and assisted Allied Forces when possible.

Following instructions, we also moved our camp inland to the village of Tankulan. We basically over took the abandoned town, living in the natives' huts. Some

*Bob Dowding on the left with Walt Regehr
and native girls selling fried bananas.*

time after March 1, 1942, we received word an important figure would be arriving at Bugo and I was instructed to return to Del Monte for a special assignment.

Soon after, General MacArthur, Commander in Chief of U.S. Forces in the Pacific, arrived on the island from his previous post on Corregidor. His stop on Mindanao was part of an escape from the Philippine islands to Australia. This was apparently his last chance to get out of the Philippines. His goal was to reach Australia and reorganize the American forces. MacArthur, his wife and child, nine generals, and assorted staff docked in a P.T. boat, which at the time was considered a state-of-the-art vessel. These fast, powerful boats were capable of launching two torpedoes.

I received word that MacArthur's staff needed a good typist, and I was selected by our officers to do the job. For the four or five days MacArthur and his party stayed on the island, I helped code and decode messages between the general and commanders in the Philippines and Australia. Of the four others who were also assisting, I was the only enlisted man participating.

During that time, I ate and slept in the room in which I worked. Nobody left the abandoned Del Monte building that had become a makeshift command center. Oddly enough, I have no recollection of the nature of the messages being sent and received. I guess I knew this information was top-secret and just erased it from my memory.

It took several days to coordinate the two planes and other logistics that would get General MacArthur safely off the island. Then, as quickly as he arrived, the renowned general departed. Before leaving, MacArthur eyed us—a makeshift bunch of men called to be soldiers—and uttered the famous quote "I shall return." Then he left to plan the next step in America's war effort.

I was later commended for my efforts by Brigadier General S. B. Akin, signal officer in the Mindanao force in the Philippines. I was cited with four others for "diligence, accuracy, quickness of learning an entirely new system, absolute reliability and effort 24 hours of each day." Those commended with me were all officers; I was the only private to earn the honor.

As General MacArthur's plane faded into the distance, those of us left at Mindano reflected on our situation.

I knew the General and his staff were leaving the island before Japanese intervention made it impossible. Food shipments from beyond the island ended after the initial bombing and any nourishment we were able to obtain came from other parts of the island. Carl Nordin and the 2nd Quartermaster Detachment were responsible for rounding up enough for us to eat.

Our defense consisted of a few antiquated rifles left behind by MacArthur's armed guards. These weapons were actually more antiques and looked like they dated back to the Spanish-American War.

I had a pretty empty feeling. It was just the Japanese and us. And so, hungry and defenseless, our wait continued.

I rejoined the rest of my group as we moved around and slept in various locations. There were many risks. Snakes and disease were always a concern, and the Japanese were moving ever closer.

And then there were the infamous Moros. The Moro were a tribe that had survived in the interior of Mindanao for many years and were known to be headhunters.

I had an opportunity to see some members of the Moros tribe during a trip to the city of Cagayan. Located about twenty miles or so from Bugo, the Filipino city had modern stores, cars, and blacktop roadways. In the middle of all this were scattered a few Moros. In addition to their ability to survive in the dense jungle, they were able to adjust quite well to what was then a modern-day city.

Clad in only a wrap-around skirt, Moros often chewed a native plant called the beetle nut. This plant, which was also a stimulant, turned their teeth a reddish color. Many carried a dagger or kris that could easily be turned on an unsuspecting victim. They had a reputation for being mean, and my companions told me to stay clear. A few Japanese and Americans undoubtedly lost their heads to this war-like jungle tribe.

Besides the physical dangers, there were also more subtle areas of concern. We had been warned in Hawaii, and again in the Philippines, that spies were an ever-present danger. We all had to be careful about what was said to whom. This only served to increase our existing sense of paranoia.

The name of the game was survival and the odds weren't in the favor of the 5th Air Base group. For seven weeks following MacArthur's departure, I don't remember doing much of anything except struggling to find food and shelter.

In March, 1942, General Wainwright was placed in charge of all the American Armed forces in the Philippines.

Our situation continued to deteriorate. The peninsula of Bataan, located on the island of Luzon (about 300 miles northeast of Bugo) saw most of the fighting and resulted in an American surrender. Then the Japanese turned their full firepower on Corregidor, a U.S. military installation just south of Bataan. When that fell as well, the Japanese commander insisted Wainwright surrender all of the American Forces in the Philippines or all Americans on Corregidor would be killed.

The General realized that nothing more could be gained by continuing the fight. Knowing the Japanese would slaughter thousands of American soldiers, Wainwright negotiated terms of surrender. He sent a member of his staff along with a Japanese officer to the Commander of the Mindanao Forces with details of the surrender.

At the onset of the war, it was thought American forces in the Philippines would be able to stave off Japanese capture for about two weeks. In spite of the overwhelming numbers and superior equipment of the Japanese, we were able to hold the Philippines for six months. It was a noteworthy accomplishment considering how few men were expected to accomplish this mission and how unprepared for war we were.

To surrender, we were to meet the Japanese forces at Camp Casising, near the city of Malaybalay on Mindanao. By this time, we had made our way well inland and were near a village called Maramag. After receiving our orders, we had to retrace our steps 75 miles northward.

It was May 8, 1942. There wasn't much time to prepare for surrender. We received word at about midnight and were to leave by truck at daybreak. A number of us considered fleeing into the jungle, but the idea quickly lost its appeal when we thought of the poisonous snakes, malaria, and distance from civilization.

We threw all of our equipment — typewriters, guns, knives, etc. — into a deep canyon near Maramag and went on to the village of Malaybalay.

My thoughts before meeting the Japanese were a mixture of anxiety and relief. In many ways, surrender meant an end to the constant stress we were under. We had no idea when we would be attacked or when a Japanese soldier would jump out from behind a tree. We also knew being held captive would be no picnic. But never having talked to a POW, we really had no idea what to expect.

Looking back, I think the months of being under so much stress affected my emotions so much that I wasn't really functioning properly. And I think it would be safe to say that up until the very end we expected the United States to send some type of reinforcements.

We were met by the Japanese at Camp Casising near Malaybalay on May 9, 1942. They were waiting for us and confiscated all watches, rings, and other valuables. We were placed in a fenced enclosure that had some native buildings we used for barracks. The Japanese had put a length of barbed wire around this old Philippine military training camp. The whole thing was very quiet and orderly. American officers were in charge of keeping POWs organized. We all gave our name, rank and serial numbers — the only information we were required to give as prisoners of war. A little later, I was called to Japanese Headquarters to type up this information for their records.

The camp contained about 1,000 American troops. I remember it to be quite primitive there. But in the tropics, the weather is always so mild there is no real need for windows or doors.

We were warned not to come within five feet of the surrounding barbed wire fence. Unfortunately, some unwitting Filipinos failed to heed this warning. The Japanese made the two men dig their own graves and were promptly killed right in front of us.

At some point, while typing up information on American captives inside Japanese headquarters, I stole a

```
6/12/42.
                Camp Malaybalay
          As I look out across the vale
         From our shack of grass and nipa
         I can see the mountains rising
          In all their gorgeous beauty

      At the foot of the hills is a town
       You can see the tin roofs glisten
      Amidst two trees of brilliant green
         It's like a beautiful picture

          Each afternoon I can see
        The rain up in the mountains
         The clouds come down so low
         They touch each hill and peak

       Some days the skies are darkened
          By countless flying hoppers
          They look like blowing snow
         Against the sky's bright blue

         I often sit around and sigh
        Wishing to get home somehow
        As I gaze out over Malaybalay
          On the Isle of Mindanao
                    - Dowding
```

This poem was composed by the author while looking out the window at Camp Malaybalay.

few minutes to write a poem. At the time, my captors apparently weren't paying much attention and assumed I was busy typing up POW forms. Somehow, I was able to save this small demonstration of personal freedom throughout my captivity. I still have the original, although how I was able to save such an item is lost to me.

The Japanese picked a group of healthy POWs with some mechanical talent and shipped them to Japan.

48

About mid-October, they decided that we all should be working in some capacity. Loading us in trucks, we were taken to the port of Bugo. Next, we boarded a boat that sailed around the Northeast part of Mindanao and then south to the large port city of Davao.

This port had been under Japanese occupation for quite some time. When we got off the ship, we were forced to walk 15 miles inland. An abandoned Philippine prison camp — complete with barbed wire fencing — then became our new home.

Sketch by an unknown POW, 1943.

In addition to members of the 5th Air Base group, soldiers from a number of other divisions were also brought into the Davao Penal Colony (also known as Dapecol). All told, there were about 1,000 of us.

At about the same time, an additional group of men arrived from Corregidor and Bataan, swelling the Davao

POW population to about 2,000. Many of these soldiers were in very bad shape. Like us, they had been short on rations for quite some time. Out of desperation, these men ate all the horses and mules at their various war time locations. The situation was made worse by the fact many had seen months of fighting prior to their capture.

To further compromise their already frail health, many were forced to participate in what became known as *The Death March*. (For more information on the Death March, see Appendix, page 116.)

During this infamous march, allied troops captured after the surrender of Bataan were forced to walk several miles to a railroad. Many fell from thirst or starvation and were promptly shot. Those who slowed to help a fellow soldier along the way were also shot. Thousands of men perished during the death march, their remains later buried in trenches along the roadside.

The Japanese commander at Davao was less than happy to see the addition of these 1,000 or so survivors. He had been hoping for strong, healthy men capable of working in the fields.

At first, none of us knew exactly what to expect at our new location. Guard towers surrounded the compound and a soldier was posted near the door of each of the seven or eight barracks.

That gave us all a pretty good idea of what we were up against and the consequences of not following orders to the T.

They warned us that if anyone attempted to escape, the ten men sleeping nearest to them would be shot. I don't know if this threat was an escape deterrent or not, but ten men finally did make a successful escape sometime early in 1943. We found out that they survived and joined guerrilla forces in the hills. I heard that about 100 men were taken out of camp and held by themselves for awhile but eventually the Japanese relented and nobody was shot.

Guards at Davao were quite different than those at Malaybalay. At the latter, many appeared to be members of the army and seemed to realize we, like they, were only doing our duties. Guards at the Davao prison, on the other hand, were very sadistic and took pleasure in hurting their prisoners.

Following World War I, a number of countries signed a code of conduct detailing how POWs should be treated. But because Japan was not a signing member of the agreement, the guards apparently felt they could do as they wished.

The Japanese immediately put us to work. An interpreter was used to communicate our instructions. We eventually got into a routine and went to do the jobs that became familiar. A few qualified men were put in the motor pool. Others worked at clearing away jungle for the La Sang airfield, which had a runway of crushed coral. There was also a small farm where vegetables and a few chickens were tended for Japanese consumption.

Many, including myself, spent a good deal of time in the rice fields. Each morning, those assigned to this task would get on a narrow-gauge railroad and travel out to the paddies.

Of all the jobs, this was one of the most tedious. A single guard was in charge of 20 or more men. They did, after all, have the guns and it was hard to visualize escaping into the jungle with nothing on but a G-string.

Some of the men thought they would fool the guards and work more slowly. However, the Japanese could easily spot a straggler in the group.

Hours would be spent in the hot sun with bare feet submerged in the mud. Seedlings were planted, tended, and harvested by hand. Everything in the Philippines at the time was primitive. And although American sweat was used in raising the rice, as POWs we seldom saw the fruits of our labors. Most of what was produced undoubtedly went to feed the Japanese as we starved. While the Japanese goal was food production, ours was staying alive.

How can I explain what it was like to go to bed hungry each night and awaken hungry in the morning? How can one imagine performing hard manual labor day after day with nothing but a pat of rice and cup of weak tea to satisfy the endless ache in our stomachs?

Much of what we were offered contained more worms than rice, but we ate them anyway because of the extra nourishment they offered. Occasionally, we would get a fish head mixed in broth. But when I would see that fish head floating with vacant eyes, it was hard to drum up much enthusiasm to eat.

If a water buffalo died, we might see it on our plates a couple of days later. Looking back, we ate a lot of stuff we shouldn't have. It's a wonder more of us didn't get sick. As it was, the most prevalent problem was severe malnutrition. Thankfully, I was small and required less food than many of my fellow prisoners.

The Japanese did allow us to have small gardens behind the barracks. We grew a few eggplants, some peppers, and various greens. We didn't really wait for these plants to produce fruit before harvesting them. We ate from them from the time they came up from the ground, using them to supplement our rice.

I gardened with a friend by the name of Abe Sabbatini. He knew a good deal more about raising things than I, but he was happy for the help I offered. Years after our captivity, Abe and I have kept in touch and remain friends today.

Amazingly, we didn't have much trouble with stealing from each other's gardens and we shared when we could.

In about mid-1943, we received a Red Cross package. This was like a gift from heaven to help us survive.

Amazingly, some of the men opted to exchange their valuable food allotment for cigarettes. The trade of food and cigarettes was a common occurrence in POW camps. In spite of this, I tended to take what I got and leave it at that. Although I was a nonsmoker, I was not about to

Form 1631-P
Feb. 1942

✚ American Red Cross
STANDARD PACKAGE NO. 8
for
PRISONER OF WAR
FOOD
CONTENTS

Evaporated Milk, irradiated	1 14½ oz. can
Lunch Biscuit (hard-tack)	1 8 oz. package
Cheese	1 8 oz. package
Instant Cocoa	1 8 oz. tin
Sardines	1 15 oz. tin
Oleomargarine (Vitamin A)	1 1 lb. tin
Corned Beef	1 12 oz. tin
Sweet Chocolate	2 5½ oz. bars
Sugar, Granulated	1 2 oz. package
Powdered orange concentrate (Vitamin C)	2 3½ oz. packages
Soup (dehydrated)	2 2½ oz. packages
Prunes	1 16 oz. package
Instant Coffee	1 4 oz. tin
Cigarettes	2 20's
Smoking Tobacco	1 2¼ oz. package

At the left is a copy of the slip that listed the items included in the package from the Red Cross.

trade my cigarettes for a portion of rice belonging to someone else. Doing so would have only brought starvation closer for them.

Poor sanitary facilities led to widespread dysentery, while others fell ill from malaria as well as malnutrition. A shallow, hand-dug well about eight to ten feet across was located in front of each of the barracks. The water was as dark as coffee and tasted like mud. This is what we used for drinking and bathing ourselves.

One problem that grew with the length of our captivity was the prevalence of bedbugs or fleas. Their bite was quite painful, and they would hide in the seams of our clothing. Our only recourse was to flip the pests out of our clothes with a fingernail. But with 2,000 men sleeping in close proximity, no true remedy for the problem existed.

There was a building at the camp we called the hospital. It was staffed by three or four medical corpsman and maybe two or three doctors. However, one had to be very sick before the Japanese permitted them in the hospital.

At the end of each day, I would be completely exhausted. One might assume that a man in his prime would think of girls. Instead, every thought centered on the ache of hunger in our bellies. We all talked about our favorite foods and probably tortured ourselves unnecessarily. Sleep brought complete darkness, unbroken by dreams.

We did get every other Sunday off — I don't think we would have been able to make it if they'd worked us every day. There were some clergy in camp, including a couple of Catholic priests. When we had a Mass, which was seldom, it was shortened significantly. The Japanese did not like us congregating for long periods of time for fear we would organize a revolt. For the most part, our Sundays off were spent resting and doing some visiting. Again, talk centered on what we would like to eat.

It was at this time some of my most enduring friendships were forged. Out of a desire for companionship, as well as survival, I became friends with fellow POWs Dwight Shaw, Walt Regehr, Ray Heimbuch, Charlie Bruce, Abe Sabbatini, Buss Cline, and Clyde Simmons. We all survived and came home.

Although there were about 2,000 in the camp, these individuals, who hailed mostly from the western United

*Above and Below: Photos of Davao Penal Colony
taken by Glenn Nordin on a return visit.*

*Photos of Davao Penal Colony
taken by Glenn Nordin on a return visit.*

States, became my support system. Our common bond was a sense of quiet hope and optimism for our survival and successful return home. We gave each other encouragement and watched each others' backs. But often, as we collapsed from exhaustion and were too tired to talk, the comfort of their presence gave the greatest peace of mind.

Associating with these select few also had other safety benefits. Although the times I spent in Japanese headquarters typing was a welcome change for me, I did not want my assignments to become common knowledge. My duties there had the possibility of creating distrust among others in camp. As far as I was concerned, the fewer people who knew about my typing job at Japanese headquarters, the better.

Having someone to rely upon helped me deal with the unbelievable difficulties of POW life. Being a prisoner was psychologically debilitating.

There were constant dangers and threats to my life. A Japanese soldier could explode in anger at any time for no apparent reason. Talking to my buddies helped me know what was going on around camp. Staying alert helped avoid behaviors that would end in a beating—or death.

One ritual we quickly became aware of was paying respect to the guards. Upon passing one, POWs were expected to bow. This was also to be done each morning and night as we passed the guard house in and out of camp. Failing to do this could result in a severe beating or kneeling before the guards for hours at a time.

After a while, I became numb to the constant fear and dealt with it by blocking it out. As a result, much of the time I spent as a POW is a blur—specific events, days, weeks, and months are forever lost. Most of my memories of my POW time are suppressed—captured in an area of my psyche where demons are unable to escape or be visited.

Sometime during 1943, and about twice after that, we were able to send a notice to our parents on preprinted cards. Guess who was lucky enough, or guided by God, to be the one to type these up?

Such jobs always kept me out of the rice fields for some time, because I didn't type very fast. I had to be very careful about the spelling of names and addresses. I felt it was important to be accurate considering the small amount of information that would fit on each card. The first postcard I sent took ten months to travel from Davao to my parents home in Seward, Nebraska.

IMPERIAL JAPANESE ARMY

1. I am interned at Philippine...

2. My health is — excellent; good; fair; poor.

3. I am — injured; sick in hospital; under treatment; not under treatment.

4. I am — improving; not improving; better; well.

5. Please see that Mom, Dad and brothers and sisters .... is taken care of.

6. (Re. Family). Dont worry about me. I'll ... OK. ... of yourselves. H..e to see you ... ..n.

7. Please give my best regards to ...Co...

One of the cards Dowding typed at Davao Penal Colony that was sent to his family in Seward, Nebraska.

Prior to that time, the friends and family I left behind knew little of my situation. In August, 1942, my parents were notified by the war department that I was listed as "missing in action" as of March 1942 — the first resident of Seward County to be classified as such. The communication carried July as the only date of confirmation. They assumed I had been killed until receiving my card in

59

WESTERN UNION

October, 1943, Dowding's parents were notified that he was a Prisoner of War held by the Japanese.

March, 1944, when they discovered I was a prisoner of war. When hearing still nothing more for almost a year, they began to assume the worst.

Things changed abruptly in June, 1944, when the Japanese decided to move us. Although I didn't know it at the time, Allied forces were getting closer to the Philippines and the Japanese were getting nervous. We had, at that time, spent two years at the Davao prison.

At about 6 A.M. we were tied in single file in a truck, blindfolded, and driven back out to coastal Davao. On this miserable journey, we were hardly able to move because of the coarse, abrasive ropes wrapped around our necks. Although I do not know for sure, the Japanese un-doubtedly feared they would be ambushed by guerrilla forces while traveling through the jungle. We were not given anything to eat or drink until reaching our destination.

When we finally arrived and the blindfolds were re-moved, we saw the first ship of three that would be our transportation to Japan. And our first impression was by no means encouraging. Everything about the old ship seemed disorganized. The rusty vessel had stacks of crates and boxes piled above deck. I wondered if such an old ship was even seaworthy.

We were quickly loaded into the hold which was di-vided into two or three compartments. It was almost dark below-deck, but our eyes eventually adjusted to make use of the little light that did eventually reach us.

We boarded until we had reached capacity, and then a few hundred more continued to come. This went on un-til about 700 or 800 POWs were aboard. There was no room to lie down, no room to sit, and barely enough room to breath.

Our conditions were not only cramped, but also un-sanitary. The bathroom facility consisted of a five-gallon bucket, and with cases of dysentery and sea sickness run-ning rampant, this was hardly sufficient.

Although we didn't know it at the time, we were destined for Japan. What we did know was that being jammed into the hold for any length of time would be miserable. Adding to that was the fact these ships were old and slow and it meant a long, unpleasant journey.

My friends and I tried to manage our fear and discomfort by sticking together. Heimbuch, Bruce, Shaw and I took turns resting by making just enough room for two to sit down and rest at a time. We tried to stay near the hatch, so that if an opportunity to go above deck came up, we would be among the first to take advantage of it.

After our ship left port, we were eventually allowed to go above-deck in shifts. This was a pleasant relief and we all tried to enjoy the full benefit of it.

I happened to be on deck when another prisoner of war, Colonel John Hugh McGee, took the drastic measure of jumping overboard.

We were about two miles offshore the west coast of Mindanao, just past the village of Zamboanga. The sun was beginning its descent, but, in spite of the fact dusk was settling in, several of us were still above deck. Suddenly, machine guns and rifles began to blast and we were quickly hustled below deck. At the time, I had no idea what was going on. Thankfully, however, we were allowed to go top side again the next day.

Amazingly, McGee survived the ensuing gunfire and made it to shore. Prior to being captured, he had served with the Philippine army at Zamboanga and so was familiar with the island's terrain. He went on to join up with guerrilla forces on the island and managed to harass the Japanese until the Americans were able to reclaim the island. This decorated WW II veteran became a

Brigadier General and wrote about his war experiences in a book entitled *Rice and Salt*.

Our old boat continued to struggle along. Afraid of submarine attacks, the Japanese ships stuck close to the coast during the day and left port at night. Finally, at the small island of Cebu, our ship stopped running entirely. We were unloaded from the ship into an area that looked like an old coal bin. We stayed there for the next two days. At night we slept without blankets on the hard, cold cement with our ever-present guards keeping us company.

We finally got loaded on another ship which was in just as bad of shape as the previous one. This one made it to Manila, where we marched from the dock area to the Bilibid Prison and stayed for about ten days. There were also a number of other American POWs there at the time. As we prepared to board yet another old ship, all of the men in our group deemed unable to work were left behind.

Among those left behind was my friend Walt Regehr. As it later turned out, American forces liberated Manila just months later. Regehr was rescued in January and made it home several months before me.

By mid-July, we left Manila and headed for Taiwan, then called Formosa, arriving about Aug. 1. On the way, we had the unpleasant experience of being caught in a typhoon.

The tropical storm lasted for a couple of days, tossing our boat about in the water unmercifully. At times, I

```
                    COPY

GENEVE 2II 22I 9 I200

DLT JAPANESE REDCROSS TOKIO


TSOII6 KINDLY TRANSMIT MESSAGE TO FOLLOWING POW

PHILIPPINES CPLS ROBERT L DOWDING QUOTE ALL WELL

BROTHERS SCHOOL DAD SISTER WORKING LOVE MOM DOWDING

UNQUOTE

                    INTERCROIXROUGE AI726
```

茶岡人關係第一一六號

昭和一九年二月九日 赤十字國際委員會 第一七二六

左記在フィリッピン俘虜ヨリ傳言相成度

「愛シ遊ル」

一宮元典兄弟皆學ス モム・ドオウドイング

ロバート・ト・L・ドオウドイング伍長殿

父姉働イティル 殿

Dowding's family sent this message which he received at Dapecol from the Japanese Red Cross on April 30, 1944.

didn't think we would ever make it through the terrible wind and rain, but we did. Once more I felt that God was helping us.

When we finally arrived on the island of Taiwan, things had calmed down considerably. There was a hose and some water on the dock, and those of us who wanted to and were able had an opportunity to get a quick bath.

We stayed in the area for three or four days. Upon departing, we were accompanied by a convoy of about 20 ships. At last, after nearly three months, we were embarking on the final leg of the most hellish journey of my life.

This final part of the trip was by far the most terrifying. We had not gone far when a submarine alert had the Japanese setting off depth charges in the area. These charges exploded at a predetermined time, which could range from minutes to hours after being released into the ocean. From within the ship's hold, we could feel the almost constant shudder as the charges randomly exploded. We figured we would probably be torpedoed at any moment by American submarines harassing Japanese ships. None of us knew if we would be the next victims. Although we ultimately weren't, it was close.

About a month later, another ship full of POWs was following the same course we had taken. However, this unfortunate vessel was torpedoed by an American sub off the west coast of Mindanao. Of the 750 on board, only 82 made it to shore.

These survivors were befriended by guerrilla forces on the island led by the same Colonel McGee I mentioned earlier. With the help of McGee, contact was made with Australia and a submarine was sent to pick up the former POWs.

Although there was initially concern about all 82 fitting on the rescue submarine, McGee insisted they all go to the meeting point to ensure as many as possible could depart the island. Amazingly, all managed to board and safely complete their journey to freedom.

Ultimately, we reached the port of Moji on September 2, 1944. Moji was located on the northern tip of the island of Kyushu, which is very near the main island of Honshu.

We finally got off the ship and stayed overnight in an old barn-like building. The next morning, we boarded a train that had the windows painted black so that we could not see out. After traveling for about 24 hours, we finally reached the town of Yokkaichi. The town turned out to be just across the bay from Nagoya on the east coast of Japan.

Getting off the train in Yokkaichi, I was greeted by an unpleasant smell similar to rotten eggs. I came to discover the smell emanated from a nearby sulfuric acid plant.

I became quite well acquainted with this plant, since I spent a good part of my time in Yokkaichi working there. The acid often left holes in my clothes, and many suffered burns to the skin. I never did discover what the sulfuric acid was used for. When I wasn't in the plant, I sometimes helped unload ships on the docks.

Our dismal situation received a jolt on December 7, 1944. On that day, a huge earthquake hit the area. Although the sulfuric acid plant sustained minimal damage, a nearby railroad was not so lucky. The tracks became twisted and broken. After that, the Japanese had us focus on repairing the damaged railway.

The earthquake was just the tip of the iceberg. Just hours after the quake, a large tidal wave smashed the coastline and flooded the entire area including our barracks. We were engulfed by the ensuing flood and more than two feet of water accumulated in our living quarters. The water went back down in a relatively short time and we began cleanup soon after.

The work and constant threats by Japanese guards were numbing. Many of the guards there were too old or disabled to be members of Japan's army and the incidents of severe beatings dropped slightly. Yet, they always carried a stick in hand, ready to knock down and stomp on any POW who didn't respond as expected.

While in Japan we were expected to speak in Japanese. Failing to respond in a quick and understandable manner, especially during close order drill, would often result in getting hit by the guard with his big stick. We learned some vital Japanese words in a hurry, not the least important of which was our roll-call number. Today, over fifty years later, I can still recite the Japanese numbers, including my own number 307. To make us learn to count quickly, we had marching practice on the beach for a time. If someone responded too slowly, the guard would march us right into the surf until we were waist deep in the water.

Being moved so far north brought climatic changes. From the heat of the tropics we went to a climate similar to Nebraska, except it never got below zero and the snowfalls left little accumulation on the ground. My bunkmates and I often huddled together to stay warm during the nights. We would put one blanket on the floor and one or two on top.

Of course, the colder weather meant fewer mosquitoes. Still, some people did experience relapses of malaria.

The work the Japanese expected of us and what we were willing and able to do made for an interesting balance. I wouldn't say we went above and beyond their demands, to be sure. On the other hand, we weren't able to do anything obvious in the way of sabotage, although I did later hear some POWs managed to undermine some Japanese efforts. We walked a fine line in many situations to stay out of trouble while not doing any more than necessary.

Our circumstances seemed hopeless. By this time, it had been three years since we'd received any news from the outside world. Weak in health and broken in spirit, many of my fellow POWs began to lose faith and become very discouraged. To lose your faith and a positive outlook in those circumstances meant almost certain death.

I dealt with this dark time mostly in private, never losing faith in God. I realized that survival was the name of the game. I tried to face one day at a time, always thinking that tomorrow would be a better day. I felt that if I could just survive another day, I might have a chance. During this time, we noticed increasing plane activity across the bay over Nagoya.

As winter gave way to the spring of 1945, one hundred fifty others and I were taken to Toyama camp number seven located on the west coast of Japan across from Tokyo. Again we traveled by rail in cars with blackened windows.

We arrived at another factory complex and were assigned to work in a scrap iron smelter. Some pushed the scrap iron from the yard into the furnace area in small railway cars. Others tended the operation of furnaces. I worked with the detail that took ingots from the furnace and laid them out to cool. The ingots were about four to six feet long and maybe eight to ten inches in diameter. We suspected they might be turned into gun barrels at a factory located elsewhere. This was heavy work for our weakened bodies.

I coped by trying not to care much about what was going on around me. The work was boring and monotonous and remained the same from dawn to dark. The guards were sure to constantly remind us of our captive status and the possibility of being killed at any time. Here we got a little soup to supplement our ration of rice.

Bob Dowding

On April 24, 1945, a brief message, apparently from one of the cards I had typed up to send home, was read by a Japanese radio announcer and broadcast over Japanese radio. The broadcast was heard world-wide because my folks said they received numerous calls and cards from short-wave radio operators who had picked up the message. They were certainly glad to get these reports. They had not heard from me since they received a card from Davao about one year earlier.

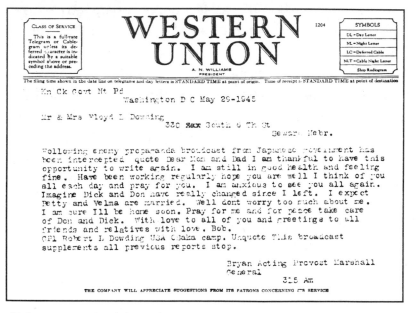

Telegram received from the Army by Dowding's family informing them that he was in Japan at Nagoya Camp, May, 1945.

The first person to contact my family was a short-wave radio operator based in Denver, Colorado by the

70

name of James Parrish. In a letter to my parents, he recounted the broadcast in some detail, although static made it impossible to decipher the whole thing. Next, a card from a G.C. Gallagher of San Francisco arrived at my parents' door. The message read:

"Dear Mother and Dad: I am in good health and getting along as good as can be expected. I hope all of you are well and am thinking of you daily. Imagine Dick and Jim are grown up by now. Anxious to see them. Are Betty and Velma married? Notify Mrs. Adele Nolty of Glendale, Penn., that her son was O.K. Do not worry about me. Send regards to relatives and friends. Hope to be with you soon again. Love to all. Bob."

This message was also transcribed by B.O. South of San Francisco, who eventually sent my parents a phonograph record of the message free of charge. Still later, a Lieutenant Commander in the Navy by the name of T. S. Hare reported hearing the same message.

In June and July of 1945, our area sustained several severe bombing raids from U.S. planes. We could see waves of aircraft spending hours attacking Toyama. These were fire-bombing raids and caused huge fires. One night we lay outside the barracks in a couple of large holes for protection. We thought these holes would become our graves. Later reports said that the town of Toyama was 95 percent destroyed.

As a prisoner, I had mixed feelings about these bombings. On one hand, it was encouraging to know American forces were close enough to put that many planes in the air over Japan. But at the same time, we really worried about where the next bomb would fall. Some of the burning debris did blow over into our area, but I don't recall anyone being injured. These raids caused considerable anxiety among the prisoners. Many thought they might be killed near the end of the war after surviving so many years of pain and suffering. But our faith continued to protect us yet another time.

I think the Japanese were pretty concerned about the effects of these raids. I'm sure many of their homes and families were burned to ashes in the fierce fires. Blown by the wind, the inferno seemed to wipe out everything.

Through it all, however, our work at the smelter went on uninterrupted and we remained in the Toyama barracks.

In early August, 1945, a lone plane flew overhead. After this happened a number of times, we concluded it was taking pictures of the damage and what might be left. We began referring to this aircraft as "photo Joe," and, after a while, ignored the flybys. Then, about one week later, we got an unexpected surprise. As we were at breakfast, heard a plane, followed by a roaring sound similar to a freight train. Somebody shouted, "It's a bomb!"

We immediately dived to the floor and took cover under the very tables where we had just been eating.

With an extraordinary amount of force, part of the building's roof was suddenly ripped off and some debris settled down on us. As we looked around, we could see the bomb had landed about 100 yards away, between our barracks and the factory. Amazingly, nobody received more than a few scratches.

The Japanese did not move us to a different location after the bombing. We continued to live and eat in the same building and our work schedules were not altered. We labored as before, going to the smelting plant and being insulted and demeaned by our captors.

Then, on August 15, 1945, we were amazed to discover we would not be going to work. The Japanese told us that something at the plant was in need of repair and would require some time to fix. The same thing happened the following day and continued for much of the week. We began to grow suspicious and wondered what was really going on.

The Japanese had told us that they had orders to kill all of the Americans if Allied troops started to land in Japan. We thought this might be the end of our attempts for survival.

Finally, American officers were called in by the Japanese commander and informed the war had ended. Almost mysteriously, all our Japanese guards disappeared. We were told to stay in camp until American forces came to get us.

Not until later did we learn the real reason for the armistice. The atomic bombs that were dropped on Hiroshima and Nagasaki wrought so much devastation and killed so many Japanese civilians that the Emperor himself decided that enough damage had been done. The surrender followed on September 2, 1945.

# RETURNING TO FREEDOM

Toward the end of August 1945, after the fighting had stopped, British and American fighter planes began flying overhead dropping food, cigarettes and newspapers. Up to that time, the last contact we had with the outside world was before we surrendered to the Japanese in 1942. The last contact I had from my family was a telegram received just before Christmas on December 23, 1941, wishing me a Happy New Year.

The biggest news in the papers was that Hitler was dead and Germany had surrendered in April, 1945. Another big news item was that President Roosevelt had died and Harry Truman was the new President of the United States.

Bombers began dropping 50-gallon barrels filled with food packages and we all sat around eating whatever we wanted.

We remained in Toyoma until September 5, 1945. We were able to go outside the camp if we stayed in the nearby area. During one outing, we saw that an American fighter pilot had crashed his plane into a power line or trees. We could see his body hanging out of the plane. By the time they were able to get him down, the pilot had died. This was a sad thing to see. With all the lives that were already lost, the passing of another innocent man during our newly-discovered peacetime was a shameful waste.

It seemed as if our rescue was taking an unnecessarily long time. To pass the time, I decided to go fishing. I traded some cigarettes to a Japanese man for a fishing line, two hooks, and a couple Japanese-made floats. I don't remember what I used for bait, but I tried fishing in a canal right outside the compound. I had no luck at first, but then I was thrilled to catch about nine carp, ranging from four to 10 inches in length. It was so nice to be able to do something I enjoyed again. It had, after all, been my first catch in four long years. In the end, I gave the fish to a couple of Japanese who were watching me. We remained in the Toyama camp until September 5, 1945, when American forces came to return us to American control. Small cargo planes called C-47s were used to ferry us out of camp. These planes weren't very large and could hold no more than fifty or sixty men. When our time to board the plane came, my POW comrades boarded in an orderly manner. We showed no fear of being left behind in the foreign land that had become our hell. We had, in fact, no emotions left at all.

After boarding the plane, we traveled to Yokohama. I remember the city looked like a tornado had passed through. Because of the fire-bombing that took place in the area, most of the wood-frame structures were completely destroyed.

We landed at Yokohama's Atsugi Air Base and were then taken to Tokyo Bay where a hospital ship lay in wait. Before boarding, we were required to take off every stitch of our clothing, throw them overboard, and be sprayed for lice. After boarding we took showers. Although bathing may seem unimportant to most people, this first shower as a free man was not one I'll ever forget. It was the first chance I had to really soap up and get clean in four years. Unless, of course, you counted standing out in the rain.

I remained on the hospital ship for several days. During that time I don't recall receiving more than a skimpy physical. Although the boat was a little cleaner than most, and had special facilities for surgery and those needing extra medical care, it was like any other. Like my trip from the states, we slept in stacked bunks. The rest of my time was spent on deck looking for people I'd lost track of and just catching up on general news.

After a week had passed, we were prepared for the plane trip back to the Philippines. This whole thing turned out to be quite an adventure, although at the time I don't think that we really realized what was going on.

Our transports were nothing more than B-24 bombers. We were seated in the bomb bay where a few planks were laid across the bomb hatch and additional planks acted as our seats. The trip was loud and a little risky. We later heard rumors of a pilot who flipped the wrong switch and caused the bay doors to open. This fatal error caused the deaths of several fine men whose hopes of returning home after years of severe treatment were never realized.

When we finally landed, our time at Luzon in the Philippines was uneventful. We mostly lay around, eating and visiting with some of our buddies coming in from other POW camps. I suspect this was a ploy to get us fattened up a bit before returning home. And we did really change fast. We went from skinny, rough-looking characters in ragged clothes to pretty decent-looking soldiers once we got into our new uniforms.

I think it's interesting that even though I gained weight, I didn't really feel much stronger. The return to full physical strength wasn't complete until after I got back home and had some time to relax and eat some good home cooking.

Back home, my parents received official word of my return to American forces. Via telegram, Acting Adjutant General Edmund F. Witsell from Washington sent the following information:

> "The secretary of war has asked me to inform you that your son, Cpl. Dowding Robert L., has been returned to military control and is

being returned to the United States within the near future. He will be given opportunity to communicate with you upon arrival."

In spite of the fact the war had been over for quite some time, we were still no closer to home. Finally, I boarded the boat that would take me back home. The ship was rather crowded and uncomfortable, but it was much better than the Japanese-sponsored trip from the Philippines to Japan. Unlike the three-month journey that took us from Davao to Cebu, Manila, Formosa, and finally Japan, our trip to the United States took just two weeks.

I docked at San Francisco in October, 1945. My return was not completely without apprehension. Having been gone for so long, I was concerned that the world I'd left behind would consider me outdated and behind the times. I felt like a stranger in my own country. I felt as though I had missed what should have been the best part of a young man's life. And then there was the remorse I felt for what I had been through and so many others did not survive. As my ship sailed beneath the Golden Gate Bridge, memories of my departure flooded back—leaving Fort Douglas, the excitement of secret mission *PLUM*. One hundred forty-five to one hundred fifty souls left Fort Douglas, Utah. Exactly four years to the month later, only forty-five were returning.

There were no counselors on hand to help us over the rough spots and bring our minds up-to-date as they have today. In fact, it wasn't until nearly 50 years later that I received psychiatric attention to heal otherwise invisible war-time scars. However, I feel as though I have fared better than young men who fought in wars since. Unlike the Vietnam War, which was viewed by the American people as a war of aggression, World War II was seen as a war of defense. Unaware of drugs, I could not use them as a crutch to escape my past. All I had was the support and appreciation of my family and the community to help me readjust.

A few original members of the 5th Air Base Group had returned to the states earlier. Bob Kirker, Hayes Bolitho, and Don Gillin had survived the sinking of their hell ship and been involved in the amazing submarine rescue from Mindanao in October, 1944. Additional members of our group were freed when U.S. forces recaptured Luzon and liberated POWs from the Bilibid Prison in Manila.

As you can imagine, keeping track of so many people during wartime is not easy to do. Some had died from illness or by accident. Others were killed in action or had just disappeared. Many soldiers experienced very rough times during the war—especially those who saw actual combat.

Between Thanksgiving Day, 1941 and September 5, 1945, members of the 5th Air Base experienced stress, malnutrition, disease, and forced labor for such an extended period of time that we suffered a death rate of about 50 percent. Since the end of World War II, the mortality rate among POWs has continued to remain higher than non-POW groups.

After we reached California, I was admitted to Letterman Hospital. The Red Cross arranged telephone calls for us to talk to our parents or family. Up to that point, they had no idea of my location or even if I was still alive. The message from Japan stating that I was a POW had been delivered six months prior to my arrival in the states. Still, after so many months of hearing nothing I think my family did worry about me. But Mom continued to have faith and walked to church every morning to pray for me.

At last, it was my turn to talk. The short visit was a particularly emotional one for all of us. I was happy to hear that everybody at home was OK and my parents were relieved to hear I was fine and back in the States. However, because many other POWs were waiting to call home, we quickly said our goodbyes.

I can remember that my friend Clyde Simmons was on the phone just before me. When he was told that his girl friend had married someone else, he was really quite blue. But when I came back to the room after my call, I told him that my girl friend had been married twice since I was gone. After being listed as "missing in action" for a year, many people assumed we were dead. Clyde and I had a good laugh over this and decided that God probably had something better in mind for us.

After about a week at Letterman, we were given leave to go home and see our folks. I left San Francisco on the Union Pacific and arrived in Grand Island, Nebraska, at 2 A.M. I had some coffee and waited around the station for the Lincoln/Billings line that would take me back to Seward.

I arrived at the Seward depot, at the bottom of Sixth Street, about 9:30 A.M. As I stepped off the train, I was amazed at how little things had changed. It seemed so odd, considering how much I had been through. Yet, as I walked the two-block stretch that would take me into the arms of my unsuspecting family, I was comforted by the simple, predictable place I called home.

After an emotional greeting with Mom, she called the post office and Dad came home for a few moments to see me. Then, he returned to complete his mail route.

I settled down to catch up on the lives of family and friends. Brothers Dick, then nine years old, and Don, age seventeen, were living at home. But my sisters, Velma and Betty, had both been married and were living out of state. Velma was in Salt Lake City where her husband, Russ Struthers, was in the Army at Fort Douglas, Utah — the very place I'd started from. Betty was living in San Diego, California and had married John Tomandl.

It didn't take long to get used to being home again. We talked about relatives and friends so that I would become aware of who was still around, who was gone, and what exciting things were going on in Seward.

In spite of the fact that World War II had wreaked havoc around the whole world, only a few of my friends and relatives were lost during the war. My cousin, Frank

Bob's family around 1960. Back row: Bob, Velma, Betty, Don and Dick. Bob's parents are seated in front.

Zeleny, was killed in France. He had gone overseas with the local National Guard Unit from Seward. He was in the infantry, had received a battlefield promotion to 1st Lieutenant, and was then killed at the Battle of the Bulge in France.

Another Seward acquaintance, Eddie Rohren, was killed in the battle of the Philippines while MacArthur was fulfilling his words "I shall return."

Sometime soon after I got back home, I found out that my old girl friend was staying with her folks in Grand Island. I knew that I had to see her just one more time to hear her say that she was married. I called her up and she invited me over for a visit and to hear about my experiences. After a nice visit with her and her folks, the two of us decided to go downtown for a soda. It was then that we had a chance to talk things over. She explained that in most cases missing in action meant the worst and she assumed I was dead. Anyway, I took her back home, told her good-bye and have never seen her since.

To help me catch up on things, I had to spend my share of time in local bars. That was the place to go to become reacquainted with what was going on in the community.

The talk in the beer joints didn't focus on the war — in fact, quite the opposite was true. Looking back, very few veterans talked about the part they played in the war effort. To this day I do not know what part Max Slonecker (the cousin I went to Lincoln with to sign up for the service) did to aid the war effort. For many it was too emotional to discuss. Even today, I have a difficult time sharing these painful memories. My experiences were so foreign to those living in the safe hamlet of Seward, Nebraska, that many would have doubted they actually took place.

Although the local people couldn't imagine my wartime experiences, everybody was very friendly. I can remember meeting up with two young ladies working at the grocery store. We ended up spending some happy times together and even today one of them, Georgia, is still a good friend.

MARTHA JOINS MY LIFE

One day after having a few beers with the boys, I left Heuman's tavern and saw a beautiful young lady looking at pictures in the window of Wilson's Studio. By then, I was past my shy stage and struck up a conversation with this beauty, whose name I quickly learned was Martha. By the time we had walked one block to the post office, I'd asked her for a date. When she said yes, I was elated.

It turned out to be quite a first date, to be sure. We decided to see a show in Milford, a town about 15 miles south of Seward. I'd borrowed my dad's car and was

fully prepared to impress Martha in whatever way I could. However, the car stopped dead in the middle of the highway, and my date ended up helping me push it off to the side of the road. We then walked to the Newton Café, which my aunt and uncle had operated for many years. Thankfully, cousin Frank was willing to take us back to Seward. So, the first date with my dream girl ended rather quickly.

Martha's graduation photo

85

Photo taken upon discharge from the army in March of 1946.

But I wouldn't accept defeat and, when I ran into her downtown about a week later, I asked her out again. Surprisingly, she said yes, and this next outing went much better.

Sometime after that, Martha asked me out—this time to the Lone Oak Steak House with her brother, Lad, and his wife, Lucille. This enjoyable evening was the first time I had eaten at a regular steak house.

Martha and I dated pretty regularly after that, seeing each other almost every day.

Sometime in January or early February, I had to report back to Fitzsimmons Hospital in Denver for further recuperation. After returning home for a couple weeks, I was ordered to go to the Santa Ana, California, base for discharge. When I arrived, however, I discovered the airbase was closed, so it was back to Fort Douglas, Utah, to the separation center. I was finally discharged from the U.S. Army on March 9, 1946, at the very place special mission *PLUM* had originated. My time as an enlisted man in the Army had lasted much longer than the three years I had committed to, and the travel was much more extensive than I ever imagined it would be. The experience would forever alter the way I viewed the world.

At Fitzsimmons hospital at the end of the war. In the back row from the left: Clyde Simmons, Buss Cline, Jim Patterson; front row from the left: Bob Dowding, Charles Bruce, Lynn Torrance.

I had made it through when so many others did not. Looking back, I often wondered, "Why me?"

To deal with this overwhelming question, I decided the best way to handle the rest of my life was to live it to the fullest. And the first step was to continue my courtship with the sweet and loving girl, Martha Vogeltanz.

We spent lots of time together and I learned that she, too, had seen what life outside of Nebraska was like. After graduating from high school, she sought employment as a housekeeper in Omaha, where she worked for the wealthy Creighton family. After about four years, Mr. Creighton passed away while Martha was caring for him. Then Mrs. Creighton decided to move to California. She wanted Martha to come along, so after a short visit home with her folks, she went to California where Mrs. Creighton was living with her niece, Mrs. Will Rogers. Soon, Mrs. Creighton and Martha moved to Laguna Beach. Here Martha started working in a war plant making electrical harnesses for airplanes. After about six months, she returned to Seward to attend the marriage of her sister and decided to stay at home.

We finally got engaged in July. I gave her a ring while we were fishing at the Bellwood Lakes. We made plans for a September 23, 1946 wedding. I then asked Martha's dad if I could marry her, and, of course, his answer was yes.

I seemed to get along well with Martha's parents. In fact, her whole family made me feel welcome and we visited them often. Martha's brother, Lad, lived on the fami-

*Martha's Family in 1951 at the time of Tom & Jennie Vogeltanz'
50th wedding anniversary. From the left: Lad, Marie, Frances,
Caroline, and Martha. Front: Tom & Jennie Vogeltanz.*

ly's rural "home place" on the Butler County line, three
miles north of Bee. Her sister, Caroline, and husband,
Nick Semin, farmed one mile east of the home place. Another sister, Frances, and her husband, Charles Pesek
lived in Brainard where Charlie was the village handy-
man. Charlie was a retired member of the Marine Corps.

Martha's other sister Marie was married to Rudy
Codr and farmed about one-half mile north of the
Staplehurst spur on highway 15. All the men enjoyed
hunting and fishing, so I fit right into their activities. All
the women were good cooks and, after four years of eat-

ing with the Japanese, I thought this had to be right next to heaven.

When the September 23 wedding date arrived, we celebrated in a way that was typical at the time, but much different from today. Back then, weddings were all-day events. Martha's mother hired a lady to do the cooking for the 100 or so guests invited. The actual ceremony took place at 9 A.M. at St. Vincent de Paul Catholic Church in Seward. From there, everyone gathered at the auditorium, where we enjoyed coffee and kolaches while visiting with our guests.

After a large dinner, the wedding party went to the photography studio and took what would be the only wedding pictures. Next, we again returned to the auditorium and our guests where we opened our presents. After supper, it was off to Bee for a wedding dance that lasted until midnight.

Afterwards, Russ and Velma took us to Lincoln and we got on a train destined for our Colorado honeymoon. We went to a resort called Sportsland Valley in Winter Park, Colorado. After about a week there, it was back to Seward and work.

On April 1, 1946, I began working as a substitute mail carrier. Fortunately, I'd taken my civil service test before joining the Army back in 1940, so I already had my foot in the door. By July 1, 1946, I was a substitute clerk-carrier. On January 1, 1950, I was appointed a regular clerk with an annual salary of $3,600. At the time, Civil Service retirement premiums were taken out of every

Bob and Martha Dowding, September 23, 1946.

check, but $300 a month was considered a fair salary in those days.

Our lives received a special blessing on July 7, 1947, when our son Joe was born and again on March 24, 1951, when daughter Judy arrived.

I kept working hard, but sometimes the schedule was not good. For some time, I worked from 11:00 A.M. to 8:00 P.M. with lunch from 1:00 P.M. to 2:00 P.M. In 1964, Postmaster William Johannes retired. There were a number of applicants for the then politically-appointed job, including myself. Prior to Johannes retirement, I had started thinking about this position and decided to get associated with the Democratic Party. Attending party functions, I met everyone I could that might someday help me.

So it happened that, on July 1, 1964, I was appointed as Acting Postmaster of Seward — PRAISE THE LORD. It took almost three more years, or until April 1, 1967, before actually being confirmed as the official Postmaster. I became involved with both postmaster organizations and eventually played a stronger role with the National League of Postmasters. In April, 1970, I became state president of the group. In April, 1972, I was named Postmaster of the Year, which was quite an honor for me. We attended many national conventions.

During my years as a postmaster, I worked on a number of extra details, such as going to all the post offices in eastern Nebraska and western Iowa to give "pep" talks to employees about participating in the Savings

Bond program. I also spent quite a few days in the Omaha District office helping on budgets and postmaster selections. I even put on a seminar for supervisors.

I guess the pressure got to be too great for me because, in mid-1975, after much thought, I decided to retire. On the last day of December 1975 , my postal career ended.

Following my retirement from the Post Office job, I worked in the real estate business with Dick Besse Insurance and Real Estate for fifteen years until 1990.

The time soon came for my son Joe to make some decisions about his life. The Vietnam War was just getting underway, and the opportunity to serve his country was at hand. In July, 1965, he decided to join the Navy and completed several missions in his military capacity.

In spite of my negative war-time experiences, I encouraged Joe to join the armed forces. Defending the United States was now in the hands of a new generation. Doing so was a responsibility, but I also viewed it as an honor.

After his tour of duty with the Navy, Joe ended up with a job at the Seward Post Office as a city letter carrier. After eighteen years as a carrier, he was appointed postmaster at Jackson, Nebraska, and is now postmaster at Bradshaw, Nebraska. Joe is still single.

Years later, our daughter Judy made a mark of a different sort. In the fall of 1969, she was crowned Nebraska Junior Miss. We accompanied her to Mobile, Alabama, for a week of sightseeing, entertainment, and, of course,

Judy as the Nebraska Junior Miss in 1969.

competition. It was a wonderful experience fondly remembered by our family.

Judy finished in 7th place in the national competition. Judy married Jeff DeRuvo in 1984. They now live in Austin, Texas, and have three children—Aaron eleven, Ariel eight, and Sophia three.

Bob and Martha's grandchildren, from the left, Ariel, Aaron and Sophia

ENJOYING FREEDOM

My life continued to be productive for me as a husband, father, and active member of the community. But the four years spent as a POW were always with me, affecting my decisions, reactions, and goals. My wartime experiences shaped the way I lived. In many ways, I believe it has helped me live better.

I have tried to live each day in thanksgiving for my safe return home. In some ways, I've done this by volunteering my time at various organizations and holding a wide variety of community offices. And I have always kept my faith and remained active in the Catholic church. At the end of this book is a full list of the activities I've had the opportunity to participate in throughout my life.

Other remnants of the war that stick with me are not so positive. I never watch wartime shows like "M*A*S*H" or "Hogan's Heroes." That is not the way it was when I was a POW, and I don't see the entertainment in such programs. Nor do I watch any violent TV shows — they are simply too upsetting.

And then there are the nightmares. In the twilight, between being asleep and awake, I sometimes still get the feeling I'm captured. Although it occurs infrequently now, it is enough to make me wake up in a sweat. I always thank God it was just a dream.

Good times have outnumbered the bad, however, and I've found time to pursue some interests close to my heart. I still enjoy fishing and, over the years, Martha

Martha and Bob caught a few fish at a local farm pond in 1996.

and I have made several trips to Canada where we tried our luck at fishing in the LaRonge area. We also started going to South Dakota for the good walleye fishing, and we took the challenge of fishing the Missouri River between

Bob caught a big catfish on the Blue River.

Chamberliln and Mobridge, with Ken and Erma Timme and Marv and Lori Entringer.

Joe and Bob Dowding won 5th place at the Gresham golf Open on June 23, 1990.

I even had enough time to start playing golf. I had played a little before retirement, but now get out every chance I can. Golf is a good game. You can get exercise, fresh air, and play with some choice companions. Most of the time I play with Leo Hain and Ken Haas.

Bob and his golfing buddies; from the left: Ken Haas, Bob, Leo Hain.

Fishing with brother Dick out on the Blue River and Lincoln Creek is a fun time for me. We usually catch catfish and carp and then put them back in the river. Dick and I have fished together for quite a few years and he always seems to catch a bigger fish, or more.

Bob and brother Dick Dowding after one of their many fishing trips.

Bob and Martha Dowding will celebrate their 50th Wedding Anniversary

Sunday, September 22, 1996 at the Seward Ag Pavilion in Seward Park

Open House from 3 to 5

Hosts will be Joe Judy, Jeff and family

Friends and family are invited to come

Please No Gifts

Martha and Bob celebrated fifty years of marriage on Sunday, September 22, 1996.

Many times, my mind wanders to questions that have no real answers. How could so many die while I managed to carry on? Was it dumb luck or fate?

I was a religious person before I left, and never felt out of place with my convictions during the war. Under the circumstances, many men became more religious. It seemed that those who believed in a higher power were also more positive thinkers. Having faith offered hope that, in the end, everything would work out.

When the questions become too much, I think of Luke 12:48 which says, "Much is required from those to whom much is given, for their responsibility is greater." And this is how I've tried to live my life — to re-pay God for sparing me. Being active in my community has been a lifetime endeavor, but one I have been happy to embrace.

Today, almost five decades after my return home, I finally feel secure enough to discuss my experiences. Looking closely at photographs taken before and after my tour of duty, I see an almost imperceptible difference in the young man that was me.

Peering deeply into the eyes of my post-war likeness lies a sense of maturity and wisdom not there before. The light of existence I fought so desperately to maintain is concealed by the realization human life is not valued by all equally. From the first moment gunfire began strafing the Del Monte airstrip, death became a reality — not just a possibility, but a probability. My photograph is the em-bodiment of survival in unsurvivable circumstances.

Through the eyes of a young man, the little town of Seward looked as though it held no promise. But those were the thoughts of one bent on excitement based on the unknown promises of places unseen.

I saw what the world had to offer, and realized that, when it came down to it, I was, in fact, just a country boy. And then, I was able to go on, thankful that I lived to enjoy the freedoms preserved, at least in a small way, through my efforts.

My country and I have experienced a great deal in the last eighty years. Presidents and politicians have come and gone. Values and the family unit have been changed forever. Among the young, a lack of patriotism and respect for the very things I helped preserve seems to prevail. Those of my generation didn't expect as much as those of today. We were children of the depression and we were used to getting by with less.

Were my efforts and those of so many others worth it? Would the many who died feel rewarded by how our freedoms are now used? Only time, and the future readers of this work, hold the answer.

If you happen to see some tears on these pages you will know that they are mine as I recall the hunger, thirst, pain, and beatings I experienced at the hands of the Japanese. The scars the war left on my heart and mind may be invisible, but will never be forgotten. Such scars will be carried forever within the souls of men like me, of whom only *A FEW SURVIVED.*

Bob and Martha's family in 1996. Back from left: Judy holding Sophia, Judy's husband Jeff, Joe; Front from left: Aaron, Martha, Bob, and Ariel.

Above Governor Kay Orr, former Governor Charles Thone and Bob Dowding, 1988.

Governor Orr awarded the POW medal shown below to Bob Dowding.

ORGANIZATIONS, ACTIVITIES, AND HONORS

National League of Postmasters; State President in 1970

Postmaster of the Year in 1972

Seward Chamber of Commerce
Served on the Board of Directors

Chairman of Concordia College Relations Committee

Seward Centennial Celebration in 1967
Served as Co-Chairman for a year of events

Promoted Post Office 100th Anniversary in 1967

Chairman of the Barbecue in the Park —
served at least 2,500

St. Vincent de Paul Catholic Church
Member of Knights of Columbus since January, 1952
Help sell Tootsie Rolls for Association of Retarded Children
Help the club clean a portion of Highway 34 each year
Served on the Church Board and Parish Council
Member of the building committee for new church
Lector/Reader for 34 years
Chairman of parish-sponsored spaghetti dinners
Assisted with pancake breakfasts

Board of directors for Seward Lumber and Fuel Corporation
— 12 years

Blue Valley Board of Realtors; President, 1980

Seward County Aging Commission Chairman and Member
1988-1991

City of Seward Aging Commission Member 1990 - 1997
Forming commission to completion of new Senior Center

50-year member of the Seward Fire Department

Community Service Award — 1994
An honor for a lifetime of service to Seward, Nebraska
and the wonderful people of the community

APPENDIX

Robert L. Dowding received no pension, disability pay, or compensation of any kind from the United States Government for these wartime experiences. In February of 1994, he submitted the following paper as an example of his sacrifice for defending his country. Since then, personnel in the Mental Health Section have been very attentive in trying to give him help. Even before he realized, they had a name for the problem which had been plaguing him—PTSD. The Dental Section has taken care of his teeth for the past fifteen years. In particular, Sue Pope has cleaned his teeth regularly several times each year.

Examples of my Stress Situations
by Robert L. Dowding C-6 994 563

Our first raid by Japanese planes—caught in an open field as Jap fighter planes came in over the tree tops with machine gun bullets kicking up dust all around you. Two of our men killed.

Watching as two men dig a grave—then the Japs shot them, just to show us what would happen to us if we didn't behave.

Constant threats to shoot and kill us. Struck by hand and stick.

Expecting us to follow commands, and to count off, in the Japanese language. Always a show of their superiority.

Imagine working barefoot and naked (only a G-string) in the rice paddies of mud and water, in a blazing sun, in the Philippines. Talk about sore feet from rice stubble, insect bites, infection.

Try a three month boat trip from the Philippines to Japan. Hundreds of men stuffed in the hold of an old ship. Not even room to lay down, very little water to drink, stifling hot, and a couple 5-gallon cans for toilet facilities. Feel the old ship shake and rattle as depth charges and torpedoes go off nearby. Several ships were sunk. No baths, haircuts, or clean clothes here. Only suffering and fear.

Imagine working in Japan in a weakened condition, suffering from malaria, malnutrition, starvation, beriberi, dysentery, etc. I worked for a while in a sulphuric acid plant where the stuff ate holes in your clothes and the fumes burned your eyes and lungs. Try bowing to the guard each day as you enter and leave the factory. If you had to go to the toilet, day or night, it was bow to the guard and ask permission, and you better do it right.

If you want to lose weight—try our 3-year diet of only rice and tea. Not even close to our American diet. No milk, no meat, no potatoes. I weighed about 98 pounds in Japan.

Can you imagine laying outside in a shallow ditch as American planes are bombing and burning the town around us? Even a few of the burning embers landed on us. This happened night after night.

At Toyama, at breakfast one morning we heard a plane coming over again but this time we heard an extra roar as we all hit the floor. The bomb landed between our building and the factory but blew off most of the roof where we were. Debris fell on us as we thought our luck had run out.

In Japan it was so cold that several men would sleep together so that we would have an extra cover and a blanket beneath us. We slept on thin straw mats on a wood floor.

Think of the mental strain of no letters from home, no newspapers to know what's happening, trying to maintain a stable and optimistic outlook on your future. How do you maintain morale? Some just gave up.

Do you know that 50% of the American Prisoners of War of Japan died in the prison camps? Out of our 5th Air Base Group of 150 men that went overseas in October 1941, only about 18 are alive today.

Do you know what the death rate was in Vietnam prison camps? Well, I think it was less than 20%. How long were any of our troops a POW in Desert Storm or Somalia? Look at the publicity and counseling they receive. We didn't even know what a counselor was.

I get very upset emotionally whenever there is a display on TV of POWs from other actions, from the war in Bosnia, from showing of "Hogan's Heros" as a POW camp. The earthquake scenes in California now brought back vivid memories of death and destruction. I seem to be quite nervous, irritable, and impatient. A high startle response.

I feel that I have earned, and suffered for, every penny you might award me. It's been a long time coming, and at age 75, my days of service to my country should be remembered.

I CERTIFY THAT THESE STATEMENT ARE TRUE AND CORRECT TO THE BEST OF MY KNOWLEDGE AND BELIEF.

Robert L. Dowding
February 1, 1994

A Few Survived

```
                    UNITED STATES ARMY FORCES IN THE FAR EAST          /rld
                    HEADQUARTERS MINDANAO FORCE
                    BUKIDNON, PHILIPPINES
                                                      March 25, 1942.
"MINDANAO EVENING HERALD"
        (This paper published through the courtesy of Air Base Headquarters,
notes by Air Base Hq personnel and Radio Section, typed by Corporal Dowding and
mimeographed through courtesy of C P R by Corporal N. Atillo.)

FROM LONDON RADIO - 8:00 AM 3/25/42
        In the Zamboanga sector of Mindanao, Fil-American troops inflicted heavy loss-
es on a Japanese motor column.
        Thirty tons of bombs was dropped on Port Moresby, New Guinea, by two waves of
Japanese bombers. Anti-aircraft kept them very high and damage was very slight.
        A large British convoy enroute to Malta was attacked by Italian naval forces
somewhere in the Mediterranean. The British naval escorts shot several torpedoes
into a large Italian battleship, and then the Italian fleet dispersed. Later the
convoy was again attacked by the Italian forces but after the British sent more
torpedoes into their midst, the Italians left. No British warships were lost. The
convoy reached Malta safely bringing large quantities of important supplies. Only
1 merchant ship in the convoy was sunk by enemy air action just off Malta.

FROM RADIO SECTION by Sgt Biss
        War Department Communiques - 3/22/42. Enemy batteries on the south shore of
Manila Bay continued to bombard our harbor defenses, concentrating their fire on
Forts Frank and Drum. One shell caused several casualties, otherwise enemy fire was
ineffective. All of our forts returned the fire. The enemy continued aggressive
action all along the front on Bataan. Four American bombers, the flying fortress
type, participated in an attack on Jap cruisers in the harbor at Rabaul, New Britain.
One Jap cruiser was sunk and another severely damaged. At Lae, New Guinea, allied
aircraft made a heavy attack on grounded enemy aircraft. Three Jap bombers and nine
fighter planes were left in flames and two bombers and three fighters damaged. The
attack was pressed home with considerable success as Japanese troops and airmen who
ran for shelter as our planes appeared were also attacked. Enemy fighters attempted
to intercept our bombers but one was shot into the sea and another damaged. In this
encounter two members of the crew of one of our bombers was injured. Another heavy
attack was made on the harbor and airdrome at Rabaul and the bombs fell in the
target area. Enemy fighters attempted to intercept our planes but failed, losing
two of their fighters. Kupang was again raided by our bombers yesterday and all
bombs fell in the target area. From all these operations only two of our aircraft
failed to return.

FROM CEBU RADIO - 3/25/42
        United States submarine action in Japanese waters the last few days sank a
7,000 ton tanker, a 5,000 ton freighter and a 6,000 ton craft. Two 2,000 ton craft
were damaged and one Jap destroyer was badly damaged and believed to have sunk.

FROM RADIO SECTION by Pfc Welcher
        The War at a Glance: A combined American and Australian Air Force destroyed
44 Japanese planes in raids over the island of Timor, New Guinea, Rabaul, New
Britain and Australia in the past three days. Twenty planes were wrecked outright.
Prime Minister of Australia praised the allied action as one of the most successful
air operations of the war in the Pacific. The Japs carried out their sixth air
raid on Port Darwin and launched a fierce air attack on the inland Australian city
```

Original newsletter front page above; back on following page.

of Katherine where the damage was negligible. The allies suffered the loss of only
two planes during the day and two bombardiers were wounded. The harbor works and
airdrome at Rabaul, New Britain, were blasted by Allied airmen. In New Guinea, Jap
ground troops were pushing through the wild and rugged Markham Valley toward Port
Moresby where the enemy air force struck heavily yesterday. A lone United States
pilot raked an entire Japanese armored column on the Burma front putting five enemy
tanks out of action. The daring airman returned to his Base unscathed despite heavy
anti-aircraft fire. The Japanese are reported to be increasing their air strength
in Burma, using 80 planes in one raid on the Southern front. Chinese squads trained to fight with little food and equipment have been moved to the Burma front to
bolster the British. British forces using American equipment have taken the iniative
against the Axis in the Martuba sector of Northern Libya. Cairo reports the
British are preparing to strike new hard blows at the Axis forces. British submarines sunk 2 Italian supply ships, 2 submarines, two schooners, and one motor
vessel carrying Axis troops in a daring raid near the Italian coast. The submarines
of the latest type, weaved through mine-fields to attack the ships with gunfire.
Air activity is growing on the Eastern front as the Russians continue their advance
against the Germans. German losses are mounting daily.
New York - Pearson and Allen said in an NBC broadcast yesterday that the airplane
production of the United States is now double that of the Axis countries.

"V" FOR VICTORY   KEEP 'EM FLYING   "ATTACK, ATTACK, ATTACK"

EMBLAZONED IN PLACE

She floats so majestically out in the breeze,
    And displays her glory with grace,
The red and the white and the blue we see,
    And the stars emblazoned in place.

Our flag, the emblem of liberty,
    Of God given freedom and peace,
The motive of our ancient chivalry,
    The flag that has caused wars to cease.

The colors that led us to victory,
    With a power that none could withstand,
As sturdy and strong as an old hickory tree,
    The flag of our native land.

This creation of cloth that Honors the dead,
    The ones who fought to preserve her;
May she always, forever, float on ahead,
    To serve the ones who deserve her.

                    By Staff Sergeant Jimmie Campbell

The following are newspaper accounts about Robert Dowding that appeared in various local newspapers (including the *Blue Valley Blade* and the *Seward County Independent)* and are included in a collection of articles compiled as a tribute to the World War II Veterans of Seward County. Permission to reprint from the Seward Senior Center and the *Seward County Independent.*

Receives Word From Son In Philippines

Mr. And Mrs. Floyd Dowding received a letter from their son Bob Dowding, who is with the Army Air Corps somewhere in the Phillippines. He states that during the first fifteen days of the war he was in a machine gun pit, and when relieved was returned to base headquarters. He says the Japs have been bombing the area where he is located, and that they have scattered the boys out in a large area so that so many of them will not be just during the raids. Shortly after he was relieved from the machine gun, he came down with Malaria Fever and was in the hospital three weeks, but stated that he was feeling much better, and was back at headquarters. He told of the native villages near there, where the natives will do the soldier's washing for him. The natives also make a doughnut which the boys sometime buy. He has been in the Philippine since November at which time he wrote from Manila.

DVD: 3/19/42

SI:3/25/42

Mr. And Mrs Floyd Dowding received word last week from their son Robert, who is somewhere in the Philippines with the American soldiers, that he was fine. The letter was written in two sections, the last being written the 12th of March. He also stated that the climate is grand and that it would be an ideal place to live if there was no war.

BVB: 4/23/42

Robert Dowding Commended

Robert Dowding, son of Mr. and Mrs. Floyd Dowding of Seward, is one of five men recently commended by Brig. General. S. B.

Bob Dowding

Akin, signal officer in the Mindanao force in the Philippines. The men were cited for "diligence, accuracy, quickness of learning an entirely new system, absolute reliability and effort 24 hours of each day." They were engaged while the advance message center was located at Del Monte, in encipherment and decipherment of all messages between the commanding general and various other headquarters. Robert is a private, while the other five being commended were all officers.

BVB: 5/21/42

Receive Word Son Missing In Action

Mr. And Mrs. Floyd Dowding received official word from the U. S. Government Tuesday of this week that their son Robert Dowding was reported missing. The communication carried only "July" as to the date of confirmation. Robert Dowding graduated from the Seward high school and was with the U. S. Army at Manila when hostilities broke out and was last heard from on Luzon Island.

BVB: 8/6/42

CPL. Robert L. Dowding Is Missing

Word was received the past week from the war department by Mr. And Mrs. Floyd Dowding that their son, CPL Robert L. Dowding, was missing. The last word from him received by his parents was that he was at Mindanao, Philippines Islands, at the time the war broke out. The word was received last Tuesday from the department, but Mr Dowding requested that no publicity be given the matter then, as it was hoped some further information might yet be received, either direct or through the department. The fact that he was reported missing, however, was given publicity in other papers. The parents are still in hopes that some word may yet be had from him, and that he is alive and safe, even though he may be a prisoner of the Japs.

Robert was born in Seward November 17th, 1918 — five days after the armistice was signed at the close of the first World war. He attended the Seward schools, and graduated from the high school in 1936.

In October, 1940, he joined the army air corps and was stationed in Omaha until May, 1941, when he was transferred to Fort Douglas, Utah. The following October he was sent overseas, landing in Manila. He was recently cited by his command-

110

ing officer for service and efficiency outside his regular line of duty, along with four other men.

Robert is the first boy from Seward to be reported missing. He was a fine young fellow, and his numerous friends join with his parents in the hope that some encouraging word may yet be had from him

SI: 8/12/42

Card 10 Months On The Way From Jap Prison Camp

Mr. And Mrs. Floyd Dowding received a card Sunday from their son Robert, who is being held a prisoner of war by the Japs, that had been ten months on its way from the prison camp to Seward. But irrespective of the length of time required to reach them, the parents were mighty glad to get the word from their son. Robert sent greetings to his dad for Father's day, and said he had received no mail since Nov. 7th, 1941; that he was anxious to get home, and to tell all hello.

SI: 3/22/44

Bobby Dowding Heard Over Short Wave From Jap Prison Captured After Fall Of Corregidor

Mr. and Mrs. Floyd Dowding have received information that leads them to believe that their son, Cpl. Robert Dowding, is alive and well in a prison camp in Japan.

Their first information was a card from James Parrish of Denver, Colo., in which he said that he heard a broadcast over the short wave radio, and that altho the static was bad he gathered the information that it was supposed to be Bobby Dowding of Seward, Nebr., talking and that he was the son of Mr. And Mrs. Floyd Dowding of Seward, Nebraska.

Next came a card from G. C. Gallagher of San Francisco, quoting the message as follows: "Short Wave Listening Post, Date, April 25, 1945. Time 8:30 a.m., Station JZ 1, Tokyo, Japan. Message for you as follows: "Dear Mother and Dad: I hope all of you are well and am thinking of you daily. Imagine Diane and Jim are grown up by now. Anxious to see them. Are Betty and Velma married? Notify Mrs. Adele Nolty of Glendale, Penn., that her son was O.K. Do not worry about me. Send regards to relatives and friends. Hope to be with you soon again. Love to all. Bob."

The message in part as received over short wave radio from

111

Bob Dowding

Cpl. Dowding, U.S.A., now interned in Osaka POW camp, Japan, was read by the announcer April 24th and transcribed by B. O. South, of San Francisco, a phonograph record, of the message was sent to the Dowdings. Mr. South informed Mr. and Mrs. Dowding that there was no charge for the record.

Wednesday another letter was received from T.S. Hare, Lt. Commander, U.S. Navy, at San Diego, stated that he and his wife made it difficult to get the message verbatim. He also informed them that the prisoners love to get snap shots from their loved ones, and that mail is the most important thing in their lives.

Bobby Dowding was captured by the Japs after the fall of Corregidor and was first kept in a prison camp there. Shortly before American troops returned to the Philippines a ship carrying prisoners of war from there to Japan was sunk, and as no further word had been received from him, it was supposed that he might have been on that ship.

Now, although it is possible that this broadcast might have been merely a Jap propaganda broadcast, there is great reason to hope that Bobby us alive in a prison camp in Japan, and that he will ultimately return to Seward.

BVB: 5/3/45

Robt. Dowding Safe in Japan

Cpl. Robert L. Dowding is alive and safe in Japan, according to a message conveying the glad tidings that came to his parents, Mr and Mrs Floyd Dowding of Seward, late Monday afternoon. A telegram from Acting Adjutant General Edmond F. Witsell at Washington, addressed to Mrs. Agnes F. Dowding, the Mother reads as follows:

"The secretary of war has asked me to inform you that your son. Cpl. Dowding, Robert L., has been returned to military control and is being returned to the United States within the near future. He will be given opportunity to communicate with you upon arrival."

Further information indicated that he was released from Toyama camp number 7, in the Nagoya district.

Robert volunteered for service Nov. 30th, 1940, before the United States entered the war, and left for overseas Oct. 27th, 1941. As a member of Genl. Wainwright's army he was surrendered and made a prisoner of war of the Japs May 26th, 1942, upon the fall of the Philippines. His parents had six postal cards from him during the time he was in a prison camp there, and on April 25th of this year, and again on May 28th, radio messages sent by him from Japan were picked up by persons on the west coast and forwarded to the parents in Seward. They brought the cheering news that he was still alive. Previously it had been reported that he may have gone down with a ship transporting prisoners from the Philippines to Japan. He has spent three years and five months as a Jap prisoner.

SI: 9/12/45

Cpl. Robert L. Dowding Back In The U.S. Military Service A Jap Prisoner Since May 7, 1942

News reached Seward Monday that Cpl. Robert Dowding had been rescued from a prison camp in Japan, and this good news traveled fast in Seward. "Bobbie" enlisted in the United States army on October 30, 1940, and was stationed in Omaha for six months after which he was transferred to Salt Lake for another six months. He left the United States with his outfit on October 27, 1941 and after a few days in Manila, was stationed at Mindanao, where he was at when hostilities broke out on December 7, 1941.

He was among those who held out until the surrender of the Philippines to the Japs on May 7, 1942.

After being taken a prisoner by the Japs, Robert was able to write only a few letters home, and after a while these communications ceased. Many thought that "Bobbie" had been on the Jap ship that was sunk as it left the Philippines, but it turned out that he had been taken to a prison camp in Japan.

Not long ago Mr. And Mrs. Floyd Dowding received several cards and letters from listeners on shortwave radios saying that they had intercepted a radio message supposed to be by Cpl. Robert Dowding of Seward, but had no authentic information had come either from him direct or thru the Red Cross.

The official word received from the United Stated army which came thru Monday was real good news, and was shared by the family and friends and neighbors alike, and is as follows: Washington, D.C., 2:10 p.m., September 10, 1945-Mrs Agnes Dowding, 330 South 6th Street, Seward, Nebraska: The Secretary of War has asked me to inform you that you son, Dowding, Cpl. Robert L., has been returned to Military control, and is being returned to the United Stated within the near future. He will be given an opportunity to communicate with you upon arrival. Signed, Edward F. Witsell, Acting The Adjutant General of the Army.

Dowding was liberated from Toyama Camp No. 7 in the Nogoya District.

BVB: 9/13/45

113

Bob Dowding

Cpl. Robert L. Dowding Writes Interesting Letter From Japan
Celebrates by Going Fishing.

Mr. And Mrs. Floyd. Dowding 330 South 6th Street Seward Nebraska, U.S.A. Toyama POW Camp No. 7 Toyama, Nippon August 30, 1945

Dearest Mom and Dad, Brothers and Sister:

Just a few lines to let you know that I am still alive and in good health. At last the war is over and what a relief after the three and one-half long years of prison life and war. Only the Good Lord had saved me and some of my buddies time and time again. I am very thankful and shall always be so. Well, I will not elaborate on any of my experiences until a later day or perhaps until I return home. We received official word of the end of the war the morning of August 15 and suspected something was up. We are still under the custody of the Japanese Army until our own forces arrive to take over, or we are delivered to our forces. Are now receiving all the rice we want and a little other food stuff. On August 27th Navy fighter planes circled this camp, and on the 29th they returned and dropped us cigarettes, magazines, a few papers and some emergency rations which we were all so glad to receive. We had seen no papers or magazines since the surrender early in 1942. Oh yes, I have not received any word

from you folks or anyone in the states since November 1941. I haven't any idea what has happened at home and am certainly anxious to hear from you . I've thought of you all every day and night and at times that was all that kept me going was to see you again. My plans for the future are very indefinite as yet, but during the months of prison I've thought a lot about getting a small farm, as have many other of the men here.

One thing that I'll always thank Dad for is that he wanted me to take clerical work. That typing has helped me a lot. Thru knowing how to type (and a little politics.) I've worked a lot of the time in Japanese and American Headquarter and been excused from a lot of work details. Although since we arrived in Japan in September 1944 I've worked at the factories regularly. Being out of contact with the outside world and penned up in small compounds for the last three and one-half years, we will probably seem old-fashioned and out of style when we return to the civilized United States. I am certainly anxious to actually contact real American soldiers. I hear they landed at Tokyo today, but don't known when we'll leave, or if they will come and get us. I don't know if this letter will ever reach you and I

114

don't have an address for a return letter, but hope that someway I shall be able to hear from you soon. I imagine Don and Dick have changed a lot and that probably Velma and Betty are married.

Oh yes, I went fishing in a canal right outside the compound this morning, but no luck. I traded two cigarettes for a fishing line and two hooks. I'll try again later. One of the fellows caught several small carp, that's all there is in the ditch. Navy planes were over again this morning and dropped medical supplies, some cigarettes and some emergency rations, very few though. Well, I could ramble on for hours about one then or another, but will not. Try to write me long letters telling me about everything as soon as you find out my address. With regards to all friend and relatives and best of love to you folks and the kids, I remain

Your wandering boy
Bob

Corporal Robert L. Dowding
ASN-17011737
Unit at time of capture—H.q. & HQ. Sq. 5th Air Base Group USAC

P.S.-Dad I caught nine fish this evening, only 4 to 10 inches long, but what a thrill. The first catch in 4 years.

The above letter was written on the back of one-half of a Japanese form sheet, the rest of the sheet was used to make the envelope.

BVB:9/20/45

Bobby Dowding On Way Home

Mr. And Mrs. Floyd Dowding received a letter from their son Robert Dowding that he had left Japan for America, and that he was writing from the Marshall Islands, where they had stopped for a time. He expects the ship to dock in San Francisco about October 8th. Bobby said that the ship is crowded and a little uncomfortable, but that the trip as a whole was much better than the Jap sponsored trip from the Philippines to Japan.

BVB: 10/4/45

Mr. and Mrs. Floyd Dowding of Seward received a telephone call Monday evening from their son, Cpl. Robert Dowding, from California. "Bobbie," who had been a Jap prisoner since the fall of the Philippines, is nearing the last lap of his return home.

BVB: 10/11/45

Official army-navy text of Jap atrocities

The joint army-navy announcement on Japanese atrocities follow:

The factual and official story of how the Japanese tortured, starved to death and sometimes wantonly murdered American and Filipino soldiers who had been taken prisoner on Bataan and Corregidor was jointly released Thursday night by the army and navy.

The facts were taken from reports made by Com. Melvyn M. McCoy, United States navy, of Indianapolis, Ind.; Lt. Col. S.M. Mellnik, coast artillery corps, of Dunmore, Pa., and Lt. Col. (then captain) William E. Dyess, air corps, of Albany, Tex. All of whom escaped from the Philippines after almost a year as Japanese prisoners. Their sworn statements included no hearsay whatever, but only facts

116

which the officers related from their own personal experience and observations. The statements have been verified from other sources. After he made his statement to the war department, Colonel Dyess was killed in a crash of his fighter plane at Burbank, Calif., while he was preparing to go back and fight the Japanese who had tortured him. Colonel Mellnik is now on duty with General MacArthur, commander McCoy is on duty in this country.

Japs don't Tell Facts.

The three officers stated that several times as many American prisoners of war have died, mostly of starvation, forced hard labor, and general brutality, as the Japanese have ever reported. At one prison camp, Camp O'Donnell, about 2,200 American prisoners died in April and May, 1942. In the camp at Cabanatuan, about 3,000 Americans had died up to the end of October, 1942. Still heavier mortality occurred among the Filipino prisoners of war at Camp O'Donnell.

While this report deals exclusively with the records of Commander McCoy, Colonel Mellnik and Colonel Dyess, other Americans known to have escaped from Japanese prison camps in the Philippines include Maj. Michiel Dobervitch of Ironton, Minn., Maj. Austin C. Shofner of Shelbyville, Tenn., Maj. Jack Hawkins of Roxton, Tenn., and Cpl. Reid Carlos Chamberlain of El Cajone, Calif., all of the U.S. Marine Corps.

The calculated Japanese campaign of brutality against the battle-spent, hungry American and Filipino soldiers on Bataan began as soon as they surrendered, with what was always thereafter known among its survivors as "The March of Death." Commander McCoy and Colonel Mellnik, who were taken at Corregidor, did not take part in this, but Colonel Dyess, who did so, said:

"Tho beaten, hungry and tired from the terrible last days of combat on Bataan, tho further resistance was hopeless, our American soldiers and their Filipino comrades in arms would not have surrendered had they known the fate in store for them."

Personal Belongings Stolen.

"The March of Death" began when thousands of prisoners were herded together at Mariveles air field on Bataan at daylight on April 10, 1942, after their surrender. Tho some had food, neither Americans nor Filipinos were permitted to eat any of it by their guards. They were searched and their personal belongings taken from them. Those who had Japanese tokens or money in their possession were beheaded.

In groups of 500 to 1,000 men, the prisoners were marched along the national road of Bataan toward San Fernando, in Pampanga province. Those marchers who still had personal belongings were stripped of them: the Japanese slapped and beat them with sticks, as they marched along without food or water on a scorchingly hot day. Colonel Dyess, in a middle group, gave this description of "The March of Death:"

"A Japanese solider took my canteen, gave the water to a horse, and threw the canteen away. We passed a Filipino prisoner of war who had been bayoneted. Men recently killed were lying along the roadside, many had been run over and flattened by Japanese trucks. Many American prisoners were forced to act as porters for military equipment. Such treatment caused the death of a sergeant in my squadron, the 21st Pursuit. Patients bombed out of a nearby hospital, half dazed and wandering about in pajamas and slippers were thrown into our marching column of prisoners. What their fate was I do not know. At ten o'clock that night we were forced to retrace our march of two hours, for no apparent reason.

Drink from Carabao Wallow.

"At midnight we were crowded into an enclosure too narrow to lie down. An officer asked permission to get water and a Japanese guard beat him with a rifle butt. Finally a Japanese officer permitted us to drink water from a nearby carabao wallow.

"Before daylight the next morning, the eleventh, we were awakened and marched down the road. Japanese trucks speeded by. A Japanese soldier swung his rifle from one of them in passing, and knocked an American prisoner unconscious beside the road.

"Thru dust clouds and blistering heat, we marched that entire day without food. We were allowed to drink dirty water from a roadside stream at noon. Some time later three officers where taken from our marching column, thrown into an automobile and driven off. I never learned what became of them. They never arrived at any of the prison camps.

"Our guards repeatedly promised us food, but never produced it. The night of the 11th, we again were searched and then the march resumed. Totally done in, American and Filipino prisoners fell out frequently, and threw themselves moaning beside the roadside. The stronger were not permitted to help the weaker. We then would hear shots behind us.

"At 3 o'clock on the morning of April 12, they shoved us into a barbed wire bull pen big enough to accommodate 200. We were 1,200 inside the pen—no room to lie down; human filth and maggots were everywhere.

Given Sun Treatment Torture.

"Thruout the 12th, we were introduced to a form of torture which came to be known as the sun treatment. We were made to sit in the boiling sun all day long without cover. We had very little water; our thirst was intense. Many of us went

118

crazy and several died. The Japanese dragged out the sick and delirious. Three Filipino and three American soldiers were buried while still alive.

"On the 13th, each of those who survived was given a mess kit of rice. We were given another full day of sun treatment. At nightfall, we were forced to resume our march. We marched without water until dawn of April 14, with one two-hour interval when we were permitted to sit beside the roadside.

"The very pace of our march itself was a torture. Sometimes we had to go very fast, with the Japanese pacing us on bicycles. At other times, we were forced to shuffle along very slowly. The muscles of my legs began to draw and each step was an agony.

Horsewhip Soldiers.

"Filipino civilians tried to help both Filipino and American soldiers by tossing us food and cigarets from windows or from behind houses. Those who were caught were beaten. The Japanese had food stores along the roadside. A United States Army colonel pointed to some of the cans of salmon and asked for food for his men. A Japanese officer picked up a can and hit the colonel in the face with it, cutting his cheek wide open. Another colonel and a brave Filipino picked up three American soldiers who had collapsed before the Japs could get to them. They placed them on a cart and started down the road toward San Fernando. The Japanese seized them as well as the soldiers, who were in a coma, and horse whipped them fiercely.

"Along the road in the province of Pampanga there are many wells. Half-crazed with thirst, six Filipino soldiers made a dash for one of the wells. All six were killed. As we passed Lubao we marched by a Filipino soldier gutted and hanging over a barbed wire fence. Late that night of the 14th we were jammed into another bull pen at San Fernando with again no room to lie down. During the night Japanese soldiers with fixed bayonets charged into the compound to terrorize the prisoners.

115 men Locked in Box Car.

"Before daylight on April 15 we were marched out and 115 of us were packed into a small narrow gauge box car. The doors were closed and locked. Movement was impossible. Many of the prisoners were suffering from diarrhea and dysentery. The heat and stench were unbearable. We all wondered if we would get out of the box car alive. At Capiz Tarlac we were taken out and given the sun treatment for three hours. Then we were marched to Camp O'Donnell, a prison camp under construction, surrounded with barbed wire and high towers, with separate inner compounds of wire. On the last leg of the journey the Japanese permitted the stronger to carry the weaker.

119

"I made that march of about 85 miles in six days on one mess kit of rice. Other Americans made 'The March of Death' in 12 days, without any food whatever. Much of the time, of course, they were given the sun treatment along the way."

12,000 Kept Week Without Food.

The prisoners taken at Corregidor, among whom were Commander McCoy and Colonel Mellnik, had no experience like the death march. But after the surrender, the 7,000 Americans and 5,000 Filipinos were concentrated in a former balloon station known as the Kindley Field garage area—by that time only a square of concrete about 100 yards to the side, with one side extending into the water of the day. The 12,000 prisoners including all the wounded who were able to walk, were kept on this concrete floor without food for a week. There was only one water spigot for the 12,000 men and a 12 hour wait to fill a canteen was the usual rule. After seven days the men received their first rations—one mess kit of rice and a can of sardines.

Filipinos Frustrate Japs.

The Corregidor prisoners were forced to march thru Manila on May 23, 1942, having previously been forced to jump out of the barges which brought them over from the island while they were still a hundred yards from the beach. Thus,

said Colonel Mellnik, "We were marched thru Manila presenting the worst appearance possible—wet bedraggled, hungry, thirsty, and many so weak from illness they could hardly stand." Commander McCoy added, however that the Japanese purpose of making this triumphal victory parade was frustrated by the friendliness of Filipino civilians.

"All during the march thru Manila," said Commander McCoy, "the heat was terrific. The weaker ones in our ranks began to stumble during the first mile. These were cuffed back into the line and made to march until they dropped. If no guards were in the immediate vicinity, the Filipinos along the route tried to revive the prisoners with ices, water and fruit. These Filipinos were severely beaten if caught by the guards."

'Captives Without Rights.'

Colonel Dyess' sworn statement declared that the Japanese officer commanding Camp O'Donnell, where the survivors of the Bataan death march were imprisoned, delivered a speech to the American and Filipino soldiers telling them that they were not prisoners of war and would not be treated as such, but were captives without rights or privileges.

There were virtually no water facilities at Camp O'Donnell. Prisoners stood in line for 6 to 10 hours to get a drink. They wore the same clothing without change for a month and a half. Colonel Dyess waited 35 days for his first bath and then had one gallon of water for it.

The principal food at Camp O'Donnell was rice. The prisoners received meat twice in two months, and then not enough to give as many as a quarter of them a piece an inch square. A few times the prisoners had comoties, an inferior type of sweet potato. Many were rotten and had to be thrown away. Prisoners themselves had to post guards to prevent the starving from eating the rotten potatoes. The intermittent ration of potato was one spoonful per man. Once or twice the prisoners received a few mango beans, a type of cow pea, a little flour to make a paste gravy for the rice, and spoonful each of coconut lard. Colonel Dyess' diet for the entire 361 days he was a prisoner of the Japanese, with the exception of some American and British Red Cross food he received, was a sort of watery juice with a little paste and rice. Some Japanese operated a black market and sold those prisoners who had money a small can of fish for five dollars.

550 men Die Daily.

After the prisoners had been at Camp O'Donnell for one week, the death rate among American soldiers was 20 a day, and among Filipino soldiers 150 a day. After two weeks the death rate had increased to 50 a day among Americans and 500 a day among Filipinos. To find men strong enough to dig graves was a problem

Shallow trenches were dug to hold ten bodies each.

"The actual conditions I find impossible to describe," Colonel Dyess' statement reads. "It is impossible from a description to visualize how horrible they really were."

One dilapidated building was set aside and called a hospital. Hundreds of men lay naked on the bare floor without covering of any kind. There was no medicine of any kind. The doctors had not even water to wash human waste from their patients. Some afflicted with dysentery remained out in the weather near the latrines until they died.

Men shrank from 200 pounds to 90. They had no buttocks. They were human skeletons.

"It was plain and simple starvation," Colonel Dyess' statement reads. "It was difficult to look at a man lying still and determine whether he was dead or alive."

The Japanese promised medicines, but never produced them. Once the Japanese allowed the Red Cross at Manila to bring in quinine. How much the prisoners never found out. The Japanese did not issue enough to cure ten cases of malaria and there were thousands.

Become Slave Laborers.

The sick as well as those merely starving were forced into labor details by the Japanese. Many times men did not return from work. By May 1, 1942, only about 20 out of every company of 200 were able to go on work details. Many died in the barracks overnight. Frequently, for no apparent reason, the prisoners were forced to line up and stand in the sun for hours.

Around June 1, the American prisoners at Camp O'Donnell were separated from their Flipino comrades in arms and moved to Cabanatuan concentration camp in Luxon. There Colonel Dyess joined Colonel Mellnik and Commander McCoy.

Conditions at Cabanatuan were slightly improved—there was adequate drinking water and muddy seepage wells provided water for bathing. Japanese brutality continued, however.

"I had been at Cabanatuan one day," Colonel Dyess' statement reads, "when a Jap came thru the barracks looting. He found a watch hidden in some equipment nearby, he punched me severely to show his feeling at the idea of a prisoner still having a watch."

Expose Jap Propaganda.

Rice remained the principal diet at Cabanatuan. On one occasion the Japanese gave the American prisoners three chickens for 500 men, and on another occasion 50 eggs for 500 men. As a result, their propaganda later told the world that American prisoners in the Philippines were being fed on chickens and eggs.

Officers were not forced to work at Cabanatuan but would volunteer to take out work details. Colonel Dyess so volunteered.

"The Japs frequently mistreated Americans working for them," his statement reads: "Once when a frail American prisoner was not digging a ditch to suit is guard, the guard grabbed the shovel from him and beat him across the back with it. The boy had to be sent to the hospital. One Jap carried a golf club and beat the men working for him the way one wouldn't beat a horse. When two Americans were caught getting food from a Filipino, they were beaten unmercifully on the face and body. After a doctor dressed their wounds, the Japs took sticks and beat them again."

Men Worked to Death.

Men were literally worked to death. It was not unusual for 20 percent of a work detail to be worked to death. In one instance, 75 percent were killed that way.

Commander McCoy reported that two American army officers and a navy officer attempted to escape from Cabanatuan, which was thickly ringed with barbed wire, and had machine gun emplacements and towers outside the wire. The officers were caught moving down a drain ditch to get under the wire.

Their Japanese captors beat them about the feet and legs till they could no longer stand, then kicked the officers and jumped on them. The next morning the three Americans, stripped to their shorts, were taken out on the road in full view of the camp, their hands were tied behind them and they were pulled up by ropes from an overhead purchase, so that they had to remain standing, but bent forward to ease the pressure on their arms.

They were kept in this position in the blazing sun for two full days. Periodically the Japanese beat them with a two-by-four, and any Filipino unlucky enough to pass that way was compelled to beat them, too. If he failed to beat them hard enough, two Japanese beat him. After two days of this, one of the officers was beheaded and the other two were shot.

Call Soldiers Vile Names.

The Japanese made every effort to humiliate their prisoners of war. They would force them to stand and call them vile names. When one older American colonel turned away from a Japanese reviling him, he was knocked unconscious with a blackjack. American flags were habitually and designedly used as rags in the Japanese kitchens.

The death rate at Cabanatuan for June and July, 1942, was 30 Americans a day, according to the sworn statements of the three officers. The rate for August, 1942, was more than 20 a day. The rate for September, 15 a day—because by that time most of the weaker men were already dead. During October, 1942, the rate ranged upward from 16 a day to 19 a day and was increasing when Colonel Dyess, Colonel Mellnix and

Commander McCoy left on Oct. 26, 1942.

By that date, 3,000 of the 12,200 army, navy and marine corps prisoners at Cabanatuan had died. There were 2,500 in the hospitals, and the American doctors doubted that any of them would live.

Majority Starved to Death.

The chief cause of death was starvation. This was definitely established by autopsies performed by both American and Japanese doctors. After it was determined that the men were starving to death, the Japanese answer was that there was no food available. There was a great abundance of food available in the Philippines at the time.

Other diseases caused indirectly by starvation were wet beriberi (in which the feet, ankles and head swell to twice their size), dry beri beri, dysentery, diarrhea, malaria, scurvy, blindness, diphtheria, yellow jaundice, and dengue fever. Several men went completely blind.

The Japanese eventually permitted the Red Cross in Manila to send medical supplies, but after they arrived they were not unpacked for many days and during this period many died. Colonel Dyess had dengue fever, yellow jaundice and later scurvy sores. His weight shrank from 175 to 130 pounds, and he was given no medicine. At 130 pounds, he was considered a fat man in the camp.

High Japanese officers regularly inspected the camp and knew of conditions. During inspections, prisoners were forced to wear their best clothes, which were rags—some men had no shirts, only trousers, and many had no shoes.

Jap General Knew Conditions.

One inspection, said Colonel Mellnik, was conducted by a Japanese general. An American lieutenant was called out to accompany the general's group. He pointed out that many officers and enlisted men were too weak to stand in the ranks.

"We have many sick here," he said courageously. The Japanese general, who spoke excellent English, asked: "Why?"

The mess barracks was nearby. The American lieutenant colonel pointed to a meal of white rice and thin carrot-top soup.

"Here is why," he said. "We are all starving."

"That will be enough," snapped the Japanese general. "Your men are not starving. They need more exercise."

The lieutenant colonel tried to say more, but Japanese guards quickly stepped in and restrained him. The Japanese general curtly turned on his heel and continued his inspection with an air of boredom and indifference.

Technical Men Sent to Japan.

The Japanese took 400 prisoners who were technical men, gave them a physical examination, issued clothes to them, and sent them to Japan to work in factories. Another shipment of 1,000 technical men for Japan was being arranged when Colonel Dyess, Colonel Mellnik, and Commander McCoy left Cabanatuan on Oct. 26, 1942. These three officers and 966 other American officers and enlisted men had been crowded into the hold of a 7,000-ton British-built freighter at Manila for shipment to Davao on the island of Mindanao, with stops at Cebu and Iloilo.

The voyage took 11 days. The hold was filthy and vermin infested. Some prisoners were lucky enough to get a place on the junk-filled, rain-swept deck. Two men died on the trip. On Nov. 7, 1942, the Americans were unloaded at Lansang Lumber company near Davao penal colony. The sun treatment for two hours followed, and then the group was forced to march more than 15 miles to the penal colony. Many were so weakened they fell by the roadside. In this instance, Japanese picked them up, threw them into trucks and carried them along.

It developed that the Japanese commanding officer at the penal colony, which in peace times had been operated for criminals by the Philippine bureau of prisons, was disturbed when he saw the condition of the Americans. He had requested ablebodied laborers. Instead, he shouted, he had been sent walking corpses.

Prisoners Put to Hard Labor.

In spite of the condition of the prisoners, they were without exception put to hard labor—chaplains, officers, and enlisted men alike. Colonel Dyess, barefooted for a month and a half, was forced to clear jungle and plow every day.

During Colonel Dyess' 361 days as a prisoner of war, he received $10 in pay from the Japanese. To get the $10 he was forced to sign a statement saying that he had received more than $250, with clothes, food, and lodging. No clothes were issued until American and British Red Cross supplies began to arrive at Davao, an event Colonel Dyess' statement describes as "the salvation of the American prisoners of war."

Food was slightly better at Davao. In addition to rice, the prisoners received once a day a small portion of mango beans, and some camotes, green papayas, cassavas, or cooking bananas. However, most of the prisoners already were suffering from beri beri and the food was not sufficient to prevent the disease from progressing. Altho oranges and lemons were abundant in the vicinity, the Japanese would not allow the prisoners to have them. The brutality of Japanese officers continued. One lieutenant habitually beat prisoners. According to the statement of Colonel Mellnik, this lieutenant had done most of his fighting at the rear when in action, and had been assigned to prison duty as a punishment. He avenged himself on the prisoners.

"Work Until Hospitalized."

The camp commandant made a speech to the prisoners shortly after their arrival.

"You have been used to a soft, easy life since your capture," he said. "All that will be different here. You will learn about hard labor. Every prisoner will continue to work until he is actually hospitalized. Punishment for malingering will be severe."

These orders were rigidly enforced. When Colonel Dyess, Colonel Mellnik and Commander McCoy escaped from Davao in April, 1943, only 1,100 of the 2,000 prisoners there were able to work.

The arrival of two Red Cross boxes for each prisoner early in 1942 caused joy beyond description among the prisoners, according to the statements of the three officers. The boxes contained chocolate bars, cheese, tinned meats and sardines, cigarets, a portion each of tea, cocoa, salt, pepper and sugar. Most important of all quinine and sulfa drugs were included.

The Red Cross supplies had been received aboard a diplomatic ship in Japan in June, 1942. The prisoners never learned why it took them seven months to reach Davao.

Murder Hospital Orderly.

A few days before Commander McCoy, Colonel Mellnik, Colonel Dyess escaped from Davao on April 4, 1943, one of the American prisoners, a hospital orderly, was wantonly murdered by a Japanese sentry.

The orderly was digging camotes, Colonel Mellnik reported, outside the hospital stockade and directly beneath a watch tower. It was an extremely hot day. He called to a fellow prisoner to toss him a canteen from the stockade. As the orderly was about to drink from the canteen, the Japanese sentry in the tower shouted at him angrily.

To show that the canteen contained only water, the orderly took it from his mouth and poured a little on the ground. Apparently because he did this, the sentry trained his rifle on him and fired. The bullet entered at the neck and shoulder and came out at the hip.

The orderly cried out: "Don't shoot me again."

The sentry fired two more bullets into the man's body. He then emptied his clip at the man inside the hospital stockade, who ran for his life and was not hit.

Lincoln Journal, 1/29/44. Used with permission.